Responsibility and Justice

In memoriam
Colin Matravers

RESPONSIBILITY AND JUSTICE

Matt Matravers

polity

First published in 2007 by Polity Press

Polity Press
65 Bridge Street
Cambridge CB2 1UR, UK

Polity Press
350 Main Street
Malden, MA 02148, USA

ISBN-10: 0-7456 2998-9
ISBN-13: 978-07456-2998-8
ISBN-10: 0-7456-2999-7 (pb)
ISBN-13: 978-07456-2999-5 (pb)

A catalogue record for this book is available from the British Library.

Typeset in 11 on 13 pt Berling
by Servis Filmsetting Ltd, Manchester
Printed in Malaysia by Alden Press Limited

The publisher has used its best endeavours to ensure that the URLs
for external websites referred to in this book are correct and active at
the time of going to press. However, the publisher has no
responsibility for the websites and can make no guarantee that a site
will remain live or that the content is or will remain appropriate.

For further information on Polity, visit our website: www.polity.co.uk

Contents

Acknowledgements   vi

1   The Many Faces of Responsibility   1
2   Thinking about Responsibility   14
3   Responsibility within Distributive Justice   65
4   Responsibility within Retributive Justice   111
5   Responsibility and Justice   140

Notes   146
References   158
Index   165

Acknowledgements

The completion of this book was made possible by the award of the Thank-Offering to Britain Fellowship by the British Academy for the year 2004–5. I am enormously grateful to the Fellows of the Academy for the Award, which gave me the time to think and write. Other academics reading this will know just how much that means.

Although the Thank-Offering Fellowship is very generous, my being on leave inevitably meant my colleagues in the Department of Politics taking on extra work. I am very grateful to them for doing so. I am also grateful to my wife, Julika; that she puts up with me at all is something I find constantly amazing. That she does so through the pains and pitfalls of the writing process is a miracle.

That York is a wonderful place in which to be a political philosopher is in no small part due to the continuing generosity of the C. and J. B. Morrell Trust, which funds research in the area (and which has done so for twenty-five years). I would like to express my thanks to the Trustees – Geoffrey Heselton, Nicholas Morrell, Margaret Morrell, and Martin Wainwright – for their support. It is also wonderful because of the people who make up the political philosophy group. Since I started thinking about the things in this book, I have enjoyed the intellectual (and social) companionship of Alex

Callinicos, David Edwards, Catriona McKinnon, Susan Mendus, Peter Nicholson, Jon Parkin, and Tim Stanton. In addition, the group has been blessed with many fine graduate students. I am very pleased to be able to thank them all.

I would also like to thank Antony Duff and an anonymous reader for Polity for helpful comments on the manuscript. In addition, I have had very useful feedback on bits of this book from numerous audiences at a variety of seminars and workshops. Louise Knight at Polity has been patient and helpful at all stages, as have her editorial assistants.

In the acknowledgements to *Justice and Punishment* I had reason to offer particular thanks to Brian Barry and Anni Parker and to John Charvet. For a variety of reasons, they have had a less intimate connection with this book than they did with that one. That said, Brian and John read, and gave extensive comments on, a complete draft of this book. I haven't, I am sure, managed to respond to, or incorporate, all their insights, but that is my fault, not theirs. However, their influence goes far beyond the comments that provide tangible evidence of their involvement. Brian and Anni managed (from New York) to continue to support me in ways that might seem insignificant to them, but that matter enormously to me. Brian's and John's ghostly philosophical voices press, query, and criticize from the back of my mind as I write. I have been very lucky in having them as teachers, mentors, and friends, and can only thank them again for everything.

My colleague Sue Mendus was also the object of particular thanks in *Justice and Punishment*. She, too, has read and commented on this book in its entirety. As ever, her comments were invaluable. She also shouldered the lion's share of the work left by me when I went on leave. It is not only for those things, though, that I want to thank her, but also and simply for being the best friend and colleague imaginable.

My uncle, Colin Matravers, died unexpectedly and suddenly while I was working on this book. One of the themes of this book is that many good and bad things happen that are down to chance, but are not matters of fairness or justice. Another theme is that they are no less important for that.

Parts of this book borrow from my 'Luck, Responsibility, and "The Jumble of Lotteries that Constitutes Human Life"', *Imprints: A Journal of Analytical Socialism* 6(1): 28–43; 'Responsibility, Luck, and the "Equality of What?" Debate', *Political Studies* 50(3): 558–72; and from 'Philosophy as Politics: Some Guesses as to the Future of Political Philosophy', in *What Philosophy Is*, ed. H. Carel and D. Gamez, London: Continuum, 2004. I am grateful to the editors and publishers for permission to use this material. I would also like to thank Richard Dawkins for permission to use the quotation at the beginning of chapter 5.

1
The Many Faces of Responsibility

1   Responsibility in Personal Judgements

Responsibility, and concepts related to it, play a significant role in people's lives: in particular, in their judgements of themselves and others. Yet, the idea of responsibility is a problematic one, and when pressed, many seemingly solid judgements of responsibility slip from our grasp. The purpose of this book is not to examine the philosophical arguments over what responsibility is, although there will have to be a certain amount of that (in particular, in chapter 2); rather, the idea is to focus on where the concept of responsibility fits in ordinary life and in thinking about questions of justice.

In our ordinary lives, judgements of responsibility play an important role. According to the philosopher Peter Strawson (1962) – whose arguments will be important later – social interaction of the kind with which we are familiar would be impossible without the notion of responsibility. To see this, consider our responses to other persons and compare them with our responses to objects, non-human animals, and so on. When a person acts in a certain way, we respond to that person with an appropriate 'reactive attitude' – gratitude, resentment, love, indignation, or whatever – as his behaviour demands. These attitudes are central in our relationships with one another and in our shared social world. Moreover, they describe responses that are qualitatively different from the ways in which we respond to things, objects, and non-human animals. We may be cross with a dog, but we cannot be indignant at its behaviour nor hope that it feels remorse. Similarly, we may be pleased when we train it to roll over on command, but we do not feel gratitude for its doing so. Indeed, the very fact that we think it appropriate to *train* a dog (and, in a different way, a child) is itself evidence of the difference in the way we take ourselves to stand to dogs (and children) on the one hand and (adult) persons on the other.

Similarly, consider what happens to one's reactions to another when judgements of responsibility change. Imagine that a person has just explained to his friend how he has bruised his toe and how much it hurts. Just as he finishes, the friend – with seeming deliberateness – steps on to the afflicted toe. The victim, as Strawson says, will feel not merely pain, but also indignation and resentment and will blame his friend for her callous behaviour. Then he realizes that the friend had in fact been inadvertently pushed by a third person and could not help but step forward on to the toe. Although the pain continues, suddenly it would be entirely inappropriate for the victim to continue to blame her, and to feel indignant and resentful towards her.

Simple examples like this can be extended to shed light on many areas of political philosophy and public policy. In particular, judgements of responsibility are importantly tied to issues of justice. This connection will be considered in what follows in relation to *both* distributive and retributive justice. Distributive justice concerns the distribution of benefits and non-punitive burdens. Retributive justice concerns the appropriateness (or otherwise) of punishment for wrongdoing (see chapters 3 and 4). Although in contemporary political philosophy these forms of justice are usually discussed separately, it is part of the argument of this book that they are usefully considered together.

So, consider two examples from the realms of distributive and retributive justice. Within distributive justice, people are sympathetic to claims based on needs or disabilities for which the claimant is not responsible. So, for example, if asked whether extra resources should be given to someone born without legs, the response is generally positive. That can be undermined, at least to a degree, if the example is changed, and the claimant's condition can be attributed to him (say, he lost his legs when pursuing an extreme sport and having been warned of the likelihood of an accident). If the example is further changed, and the claimant asks for extra resources in order to satisfy what is thought to be merely a 'preference' (say, he asks for extra resources to allow him to fulfil a life's ambition of sailing around the world), then people's reactions change, too, and few think the claim one of justice (for a discussion of what social scientists find when they ask people about social justice, and many useful references, see Miller 1999: ch. 3).

Within retributive justice, notions of responsibility lie at the heart of the criminal law, and popular opinion seems in general to be sensitive to issues of responsibility in a way that mirrors the distributive case. Thus, the more the responsibility of the offender is called into question, the less people are inclined to hold him to account and to punish him severely. Moreover, many of the excuses recognized by the criminal law, which enjoy popular support, revolve around responsibility. Thus, consider a case (in many ways similar to the simple example of the two friends given above) of a driver who appears at first to behave recklessly, to veer at high speed across the road, and to cause an accident. If we then discover that the driver suffered from an uncontrollable spasm caused by a medical condition of which he was (reasonably) unaware, then our initial view will change, and he will be exempt from ordinary negative reactive attitudes (and criminal liability).

My plan in the course of this book is, in part, to discuss the great importance that the idea of responsibility seemingly has for us whilst emphasizing how seldom we feel any great confidence in our own judgements of it. It is, therefore, worth saying something about why the idea of responsibility continues to have such a tenacious grip on the practices and intuitions of people living in countries such as the UK and the USA despite all its difficulties.[1] One (no doubt, partial) explanation appeals to the Christian foundations of Western civilization. A significant part of Christianity emphasizes the will, and the importance of free choice, in human life.[2] Moreover, it focuses on the intent of the acting subject, rather than on the outcome of the action. In the philosophical form given to this by Immanuel Kant, our assessments of ourselves and of others – and, in so far as possible, what happens to us and how people think of us – ought to depend on how we choose and what we do voluntarily (what we are responsible for) and not on luck, contingency, or on things that happen to us (cf. Nagel 1979). It is in this sense that the idea of responsibility seems to be tied to our idea of ourselves as *agents*. To be responsible, as Strawson makes clear, is to be the kind of thing – an agent – that can be held to account, blamed, praised, resented, and so on. And to think of ourselves as agents is central to our self-understanding. Consider how deeply the following passage speaks to us:

> I wish my life and decisions to depend on myself, not on external forces of whatever kind. I wish to be the instrument of my own, not of other men's, acts of will. I wish to be a subject, not an object; to be moved by reasons, by conscious purposes, which are my own, not by causes which affect me, as it were, from the outside. I wish to be . . . a doer – deciding, not being decided for, self-directed and not acted upon by external nature or by other men as if I were a thing, or an animal . . . I wish, above all, to be conscious of myself as a thinking, willing, active being, bearing responsibility for my choices and able to explain them by references to my own ideas and purposes. (Berlin 1969: 131)

Of course, not everyone's background is Kantian or Christian (Isaiah Berlin, the author of the passage above, was Jewish), and the idea of responsibility is hardly unique to this tradition. The point is rather that in the countries with which this book will be primarily concerned I think it is fair to say that the idea of responsibility is, as indicated by the brief discussion above, deeply rooted in our lives, practices, and moral intuitions. Yet, for all that, when we use the idea of responsibility, we often do so in ways that are problematic. That is what this book is about.

2   The Politics of Responsibility

Although the notion of responsibility is ubiquitous in ordinary life, it has not always featured as prominently in politics as it does today. Much of the twentieth century in the UK, and to a lesser extent in the USA (that is, roughly from the rise of the welfare state in the UK and the New Deal in the USA to the 1970s), was marked by a broadly welfarist managerialism in which an optimistic belief flourished that the State could, and should, manage social policy for the greater good of all. Many of those who broke the law, for example, were thought of as the products of inadequate socialization to be rehabilitated (cf. Garland 2001) and whose prevalence could be reduced by better social policy (better housing, after-school clubs, and so on). The British welfare state and the New Deal in the USA ushered in welfare benefits for the unemployed and the indigent. Although it is dangerous to talk of 'turning points' – and social policy and political cultures are complex mixes of the old and the new – the political climate changed significantly in the 1970s, culminating in the electoral successes of Margaret Thatcher in 1979 in the UK and Ronald Reagan in 1980 in the USA. In their politics, and in the politics of the centre-left governments of Bill Clinton and Tony Blair that followed, the notion of individual responsibility took centre stage.

In the politics of distributive justice of the last thirty years (that is, since the change described above), the rise of responsibility has been most apparent in the decisions, and rhetoric, governing welfare and social security. Although this is obviously a complex area – and there are important differences between the UK and the USA – it is nevertheless possible to discern some common themes. These include two criticisms of welfare systems: first, that social security has for too long taxed the hard-working and ambitious to subsidize the indolent and lazy. The complaint here is that the welfare state has been poor at, or has deliberately avoided, distinguishing between those whose need for unemployment insurance, welfare, or social security payments is a result of their own poor choices and those for whom this need is a result of bad luck or other circumstances over which they had little or no control. Second, welfare and social security programmes are seen as providing the poor with the wrong incentives; encouraging them to become dependent on state aid instead of going out and seeking work or seeking to improve their own situations.

This diagnosis of the ills of the welfare state depends on giving individual responsibility a central place in the analysis. The first problem explicitly leans on a distinction between what was once called 'the deserving and the undeserving poor', understood as being a distinction between those responsible for their poverty and so not, in justice, entitled to help, and those whose poverty is the result of circumstance and who are, therefore, justly entitled to help. In the second, the issue is that welfare and social security payments undermine personal responsibility, and so give the poor reason to remain indolent and dependent. Thus, pundits like Charles Murray in the United States and 'think tanks' like the Adam Smith Institute in the UK have been influential in claiming, amongst other things, that state aid only perpetuates dependency and a ghetto underclass culture that invariably looks to the State to cure its problems rather than addressing them itself. What is needed, they argue, is a reorienting of state aid and a rejuvenation of those virtues that promote self-sufficiency.[3]

In response to this diagnosis of the ills of the welfare state, the 'cure' envisaged by governments of both the left and the right on both sides of the Atlantic has been to introduce reforms to the welfare and social security systems; reforms which emphasize the responsibilities of the recipients and which, in theory at least, would target help to those who, as the saying goes, are willing to help themselves. The most explicit manifestation of this has been the rise of 'workfare' programmes in both the UK and the USA.

Thus, in the late 1990s, the British Chancellor of the Exchequer, Gordon Brown, pursued a number of policies under the umbrella slogan 'Work as the route to opportunity'. In 1996, in the USA, the Clinton administration passed the Personal Responsibility and Work Opportunity Reconciliation Act. This placed limits on the period in which welfare recipients could claim benefits, and required recipients to take work in order to be eligible for social security payments. The argument offered by advocates of the Act was that those who were capable of work should only have their income publicly subsidized if they were willing to support themselves. In contrast, it was argued, those who were unwilling to work, or who engaged in self-destructive behaviour, had no legitimate claim on the public purse.

It is worth noting that included in 'self-destructive behaviour' is the having of a child by a lone parent. In both countries, then, the underlying thought was to redefine welfare and social security so as to distinguish between those for whom work was not a possibility (for example, the seriously disabled and seriously mentally ill) and those for whom it was. In the case of the latter, state aid was envisaged as temporary and as geared towards equipping the recipient with the skills to find work and sustain him or herself; an idea captured in a Labour slogan of which Tony Blair was particularly fond that welfare was 'a hand up not a hand out'. What is clearly implied, of course, is that those who are able to work, but after some time still do not do so, are responsible for their condition (they are 'self-destructive' or 'unwilling', as against 'unlucky' or 'unable'). In short, for both Reagan and Thatcher, and for their successors, the virtues to be extolled and promoted are those of 'hard work, self-help, and the acceptance of responsibility for self and family' (Deacon 2000: 15).

A parallel story can be told within the realm of retributive justice. The 'penal welfarism' (Garland 2001: ch. 2) of the post-war era has largely been either eradicated or, where it persists, is an embarrassment to politicians. So much so that John Major, the Conservative Prime Minister who succeeded Mrs Thatcher, could make political capital out of the slogan

'Society needs to condemn a little more and understand a little less'. The Labour Government, although elected to be what Tony Blair called 'tough on crime, tough on the causes of crime', has followed suit and introduced some of the most Draconian laws and mandatory sentences ever seen in England and Wales. Similarly, in the USA, politicians vie to be the most punitive; the current President, George W. Bush, takes pride in his record (as Governor of Texas) of refusing to commute death sentences; and the successful Democratic candidate for President in 1992, Bill Clinton, very publicly took time out of his campaign to oversee the execution of a mentally sub-normal offender.[4]

The consequences of the 'get tough' rhetoric are most easily seen in imprisonment rates in the UK and the USA. For most of the twentieth century the number of people in custody in the USA as a proportion of the general population ran at around 110 per 100,000. It began to climb in the 1970s, and the rate of growth accelerated considerably in the 1990s. There are now more than 700 people in prison per 100,000 of the population (if one includes inmates in local gaols). In the UK the situation is more complex. The prison population has increased dramatically in recent years, but only since 1992. Moreover, the picture is different in Scotland, where incarceration rates have remained relatively stable. That said, it is worth noting that the UK now imprisons around 140 people per 100,000, putting it a long way behind the USA, but sufficiently ahead of the rest of Europe to allow the conclusion that the UK central government has largely followed the US's lead (cf. Garland 2001).[5]

Although these figures are shocking, and become even more so if broken down by race,[6] they do not tell a straightforward story about the political significance of the idea of responsibility. In part, increasing prison rates have been the consequence of a competition between politicians to cash in on the electoral appeal of being tough on crime that has increased as the fear of crime has increased. The role played by the idea of responsibility becomes more clear in looking at the language in which offenders are portrayed and criminal justice policies justified.

Tony Blair's slogan, which turned out to mean 'tough on criminals, whilst talking about being tough on the causes of crime',
and John Major's injunction to condemn, reflect a change in
the way in which crime and criminals are portrayed in relation
to their backgrounds. Offenders are no longer seen as the
unfortunate products of bad social background, but presented
(and demonized) in individualist terms. This is particularly
true of sex offenders, paedophiles, and repeat offenders who
are described as 'predatory' and 'evil'.

This focus on the offender as a responsible agent, and away
from the context in which offences and offenders occur,
emerges also in the public's and politicians' attitudes towards
negative fault requirements. For example, in 1998 changes to
the law in England and Wales, which elicited little public reaction, effectively ended the common law presumption of *doli
incapax*, which applied to children under 14, and set the
minimum age of criminal responsibility at 10 (Ashworth
1999: 211). In the USA, twenty-one juvenile offender execu-
tions have occurred since the death penalty was reinstated in
thirty-eight states beginning in 1976. The last six took place
in Texas, and each involved an African American inmate.[7] The
trend is probably best captured by the title of the British government's 1997 White Paper (Bill): No More Excuses.

In the UK and the USA, then, the notion of individual
responsibility has taken centre stage in the public rhetoric
and public policies of governments of both political persua-
sions. In particular, in welfare and social security, and in the
criminal justice system, the language has shifted from structural and welfarist vocabularies to vocabularies of individual
responsibility, hard work, self-help, and so on. The 'third way'
– which its supporters would characterize as the recent
attempt to find an alternative to both rampant capitalist indi-
vidualism and traditional socialism and its detractors as
a means by which the centre-left can pay lip service to equality without actually doing anything about it – has enjoyed
support on both sides of the Atlantic (even if the label has
largely disappeared). Its proponents and critics both agree
that one of the things that defines it is an emphasis on what

the rhetoric describes as individual responsibility within the community. In welfare and social security policy, and in criminal justice, what this has led to is an increasing focus on the individual, rather than the social factors that surround him; to accept that the Government has some responsibility for the latter, but to emphasize that this does not excuse, mitigate, or undermine the responsibility of the person.[8]

The purpose of this book is to examine the notion of responsibility and the uses to which it has been put. One reason for so doing is that, for all its public prominence and its significance in our ordinary lives, the idea of responsibility is deeply problematic. This is not just a philosophical claim (after all, most concepts turn out to be deeply problematic in the hands of philosophers). Even in our everyday judgements and interactions we reveal that we are unsure of the nature of responsibility and perplexed by our own intuitions.

Consider again two cases: one from each of the domains of justice on which this book will focus. I noted above that people are generally supportive of claims from those they perceive to be disadvantaged by things for which they cannot be held responsible. They are also sympathetic to claims based on desert. Responsibility seems to play a significant role in these responses. In short, claims for compensation, or support, for things that have resulted from bad luck or for things that can be conceived of as needs for which the needy cannot be held responsible receive a more sympathetic hearing than do similar claims for support where the 'need' can be interpreted as a mere preference or the outcome of poor choice. Yet, actually distinguishing between these kinds of things is difficult. Thus, there are complicated debates over whether, and if so in what circumstances, cosmetic surgery should be provided at public expense. It might seem easy (at least for British readers) in the case of someone disfigured by a fire, but what of someone who claims his life to be significantly impaired by hair loss? Similarly, debate rages about such things as abortion and the expensive medical interventions that allow women to have children later in life (after they have established themselves in their careers). Again, if we treat those with depression at public expense, then should we provide those who are just grumpy and unable to get pleasure from the ordinary things in life with more resources to compensate for their 'conditions'? The list of questions and examples can be expanded almost indefinitely (and examples will play an important part in the chapters below). The point here is just to indicate how, and in what ways, our ordinary convictions about responsibility can come under pressure.

Similarly, in retributive justice, it is often said that the recent hardening of criminal justice policies briefly described above is the result of politicians responding to popular punitiveness. Whilst there is truth in that – and although punitiveness is an extremely hard thing to measure, it does seem as if the general population is more punitive now than it was thirty years ago – it is also true that politicians systematically overestimate the level of punitiveness in their constituents. What is particularly telling is that the more a person knows about the offender and his life and circumstances, the less punitive the response is likely to be. Initial judgements that 'murderers are evil and deserve to be locked up for life' often prove less stable than they seem once the murderer is identified, his life story told, and the circumstances surrounding the crime explained. More generally, debates over provocation (and over battered woman syndrome), the age at which a person can be tried 'as an adult', the culpability of schizophrenic and other disordered offenders, and the relevance (if any) of an offender's history (which might include such things as childhood abuse) to his culpability, all manifest both the importance of, and the confusions in, our ideas of responsibility (these themes are pursued in chapter 4).

3 Method

I said above that my concern in this book is not to examine philosophical accounts of responsibility, but rather to look at where the idea fits in theories and practices of justice. Whilst that is true, the next chapter will be concerned – albeit fairly broadly – with philosophical thinking about responsibility. The reason for this is that understanding why, and in what ways, our thinking about responsibility is confused (and confusing) requires that we understand, at least in general terms, what we are doing when we ascribe responsibility to someone for something. As it happens, there is no agreement in the philosophical community about the necessary and sufficient conditions for holding someone responsible, but that is not to say that philosophy can be of no help. Quite the reverse. What we will see as the book proceeds is that responsibility has many faces, and that the controversies that rage within academic philosophy mirror the different uses to which the idea is put. Knowing what sense of responsibility is being invoked when is crucial if we are to understand, and evaluate, its use in any instance.

Having provided a brief survey of thinking about responsibility in the next chapter, chapters 3 and 4 examine, and analyse, the uses to which the idea has been put in distributive and retributive justice respectively. These two chapters, together with chapter 2, offer (I hope) a reasonable introduction to some of the main debates in the recent literature. However, two cautionary notes are worth adding.

First, although the chapters cover a great deal of ground, they are by no means (and are not meant to be) exhaustive. To give a complete account of the role of responsibility in distributive and retributive justice would require the giving of complete theories of justice in both domains. It would be folly to try to do that in a short book (or, indeed, in *a* book of any plausible length). Second, and connectedly, the chapters are neither disinterested nor (I hope) dispassionate. What is presented is a particular view of the role of responsibility within justice. The argument is meant to be suggestive; the reader is asked to look at things in a particular way and to see whether by doing so various issues become clearer, more consistent, sometimes more problematic, and so on.

What is suggested is threefold. First, those who think about moral, political, and legal philosophy and practice should take seriously the challenge posed by our increasingly naturalistic understanding of the world and the place of human agency within it. Second, distributive and retributive justice are more closely related than is often thought. This is important, because those who have thought about issues of distributive justice have (rightly) become sensitive to the extraordinary difficulty of giving a defensible responsibility-, or desert-, based account of distributive justice. Such sensitivity is much more rare in the case of retributive justice, and distributive theorists have sometimes indicated that they think this is rightly so, and that the place of responsibility is much easier to discern in the retributive sphere. I want to suggest otherwise, and in doing so pursue my third theme: which is that, for those (politicians and philosophers) who believe in the equality of human beings, the role of responsibility within justice is secondary. Ideas of responsibility (and desert) should not ground our practices of (distributive or retributive) justice. The following chapters try to establish why this is so; to understand quite what it means; and to suggest how it might make it easier for us to maintain a commitment to the kind of responsibility that matters (politically and legally) in the face of an ordered, or chaotic, causal universe.

2
Thinking about Responsibility

1 Introduction

The idea of responsibility has been the subject of philosophical study and argument for about as long as philosophy has existed. In one form it appears in the debate over free will and determinism. This is briefly discussed below when the reasons why responsibility seems threatened are canvassed. In addition, there is now an entire literature on the idea of moral responsibility, also briefly described below, and a separate, but overlapping, literature on the idea of autonomy.

As this is a long chapter, it may be useful to give a brief account of its structure. The main concerns of this book are in the fields of political and legal philosophy, and in these the idea of responsibility has had a central role. Each is the subject of a separate chapter below, so here the goal is merely to indicate the importance of responsibility in these areas. Section 2 describes something of the experience of responsibility and some of the ways in which judgements of responsibility can seem to be unstable. Section 3 then describes two threats to responsibility that may account for this instability: the absence of alternative possibilities and the absence of real freedom. The compatibilist response to these threats is covered in section 4. Having argued that compatibilist theories face a number of difficulties in giving an account of responsibility that is robust enough to underpin our moral and political judgements, section 5 offers an alternative strategy that focuses on the different contexts in which judgements of responsibility are made. It is this strategy that is then pursued in the next two chapters (on distributive and retributive justice respectively).

In Anglo-American analytic political philosophy, responsibility has recently been the subject of much discussion because of the resurgence in the study of social justice following the 1971 publication of John Rawls's *A Theory of Justice*. Justice concerns giving to people what is due to them. *Social* justice concerns the way in which the institutions of what Rawls called 'the basic structure of society' (1971: 55) govern the distribution of the benefits (for example, rights, liberties, income, and wealth) and (non-punitive) burdens (for example, taxes) of that society to those due them.

Given a starting assumption that all (or at least, all mentally competent adult) members of a given society are of equal moral worth (an assumption that might also be taken to hold for all human beings) then it seems that the burden of proof falls on those who would wish to justify movements away from an equal distribution of goods. Of course, political philosophy (and practice) is awash with attempts to do just that. Inequalities have been justified on the basis of a denial of the starting assumption of equality (Plato and, in a different way, Nietzsche believed that people were of fundamentally different kinds, some more valuable than others). They have also been justified by those who accept the starting assumption of equality, but believe, like Robert Nozick (1974), that inequalities in holdings amongst fundamentally equal beings can be justified by the history of the goods in question (they were legitimately acquired and voluntarily transferred), or by the different contributions made by different people to the creation of those goods (those who work hardest in the production of some good should be rewarded with a greater share of that good than those who contributed less), or by the different needs that people have. And these are only a few of the theories that have been offered to justify inegalitarian distributions of the many and various goods that society has to offer.

Amongst liberal egalitarians – for reasons that will be discussed in chapter 3 – the most common contemporary account of justified inequality appeals to the distinction between inequalities that arise from luck and those that arise from the actions of people for which they are responsible. In the words of the political philosopher, Brian Barry:

> A just society is one whose institutions honour two principles of distribution. One is a principle of compensation. It says that the institutions of a society should operate in such a way as to counteract the effects of good or bad fortune. . . . The other principle is one of personal responsibility. It says that social arrangements should be such that people finish up with the outcomes of their voluntary acts. (Barry 1991: 142)

As Barry makes clear, this puts the idea of responsibility at the very heart of discussions of justice, and note that this remains true even if it turns out that people are not responsible for very much that matters and so justified inequalities are very small.[1] Yet, as another philosopher, Susan Hurley, has recently remarked, 'while the luck-neutralizing account [of justice] gives responsibility a central role in distributive justice, it has not focused much analysis on responsibility itself' (Hurley 2003: 1; see also Matravers 2002a, 2002b).

In legal philosophy, discussions of responsibility have been much more established as a central part of the discipline. The criminal law, in particular, has a concern with responsibility at its very heart, and so arguments over, say, criminal liability, intention, excuses, and mitigations have often dealt explicitly with (the law's view of) responsibility. In recent years, for example, arguments have raged over a number of possible new excuses (that is, over new claims that an agent may be wholly or partially not responsible for some action or event). One recent list offers 'drug and alcohol addiction, gambling addiction, brainwashing (undue influence); battered woman and premenstrual syndromes; post-traumatic stress disorder; genetic disorder; alien cultural beliefs; rotten social background' (Golding 2005). No jurisdiction recognizes all of those (in fact, very few are recognized anywhere); yet in many countries *sentencing* guidelines and practices accept the relevance of similar claims across a range of crimes. Put bluntly, we do not think that the culpability of all offenders is equal, such that they deserve equal punishment for equal acts whatever their capacity for reason and responsibility (above the minimal legal requirements for liability) at the time the offence was committed.

More generally, there have been important debates in the philosophy of law about the relationship of moral and legal responsibility. One of the most important jurists of recent years, Joel Feinberg, for example, has argued that legal responsibility is importantly quite distinct from moral responsibility. One reason for this is that legal responsibility has to be defined, and often an exact line has to be drawn – dividing those deemed responsible from those deemed not to be so – where no such exactness exists. In this sense, Feinberg argues, legal responsibility can be arbitrary, whereas that is not true of moral responsibility (Feinberg 1970).

2   Experiencing Responsibility

Part of the point of chapter 1 was to indicate the importance of judgements of responsibility in our lives. The importance of the concept in both political and legal philosophy is indicated above (and will be discussed further in the chapters that follow). Yet, the debate over responsibility has often been driven by doubts about its very possibility. Indeed, as we shall see below, a number of philosophers (and others), both past and present, have confidently predicted that the idea of moral responsibility would disappear from the languages of respectable professions like the law and philosophy. Many of these write from within the utilitarian tradition. For utilitarians, the job of government is to secure 'the greatest happiness for the greatest number'. For some within utilitarianism, this means that social policies that ignore the agency of those affected can be legitimate. As Bentham, the founder of utilitarianism, put it, 'call them men, call them monks, call them soldiers, call them machines; I care not so long as they be happy ones' (Bentham, quoted in Ryan 1987: 33).

Assaults on responsibility can come from two directions, and this is true, too, of those attacks that emerge from within utilitarianism. Thus, in the early 1960s, two utilitarian writers prophesied that responsibility would, in the words of one of them, 'wither away' (Wootton 1963), but for very different reasons. In an influential paper, the philosopher J. J. C. Smart (1961) argued that the idea of responsibility as normally understood rested on a confused metaphysics. For Smart, since persons act as a result of causes that can be tracked back to before they were born (and over many of which the agent has no control), the idea of responsibility (and of agency in the Kantian sense) is self-contradictory. For Smart, we might deploy praise and blame – which, to avoid confusion, he would rather call 'praise' and 'dispraise' – but only because it may be useful to do so. Thus, in contrast to the Strawsonian position described in chapter 1, for Smart our relations with other adult persons are relevantly like our relationships with our pets and our children. I praise my 3-year-old daughter when she does the right thing, not because I believe she is a morally responsible agent who deserves to be praised, but because I want to encourage her to do the right thing again. Perhaps more tellingly, I do not blame her when she behaves badly – she is, after all, only 3 – but I nevertheless express what seems like blame (what is, in fact, dispraise) in order to discourage her from acting in a similar way in the future. For Smart, this is the only legitimate use of moral responsibility and cognate concepts like praise and blame.[2]

Barbara Wootton – who as Lady Wootton was a hugely influential public figure – comes to similar conclusions to Smart (that it makes sense to talk of responsibility only where it is useful to do so), but not as a result of metaphysical reflections.[3] Indeed, according to Wootton, 'the real difference between the psychiatric and the legal approach [to wrongdoers] has nothing to do with free will and determinism' (Wootton 1963: 79).

Rather, Wootton argues, we have to ask ourselves what the criminal law is for; what we are trying to achieve. Since, according to Wootton, scientific and psychiatric developments have made it impossible to keep 'a clear line between the wicked and the weak-minded' (Wootton 1963: 73), she argues that the purpose of the criminal trial should be simply to discover who did what, and in cases where someone has done something wrong, the purpose of sentencing should be to hand the offender over to those who would attempt to modify his personality, or where that fails, to those who would incarcerate him for the general good (Wootton's arguments are further considered in chapter 4). In short, those who favour the withering away of the traditional notion of responsibility do so, according to Wootton, *not* because of their metaphysical commitments (*pace* Smart), but because in their view the purpose of the criminal process is not 'to punish the wrongdoer', but (where possible) 'to set him on the road to virtue' (Wootton 1963: 79).

For some writers, then, the idea of responsibility has an important place in securing human welfare by being part of a forward-looking policy that gives weight only to the consequences of praising, dispraising, holding responsible, and so on. One theme that often emerges in this approach is an attack on those who argue to retain a traditional conception of responsibility as mythmakers who retain their beliefs only by ignoring developments in the sciences ('modern biology and psychology', as Smart (1961: 291) puts it). It is as if they expect the traditional idea of responsibility to wither away just as have the medieval criminal trials of non-human animals (such as pigs). Yet, many people baulk at the conclusions of writers like Smart and Wootton. Part of the reason is that they fear the implications of a system that, for example, conceives of criminals as maladjusted and hands them over not to gaolers for punishment, but to psychiatrists for personality readjustment. Indeed, this dystopian vision underpins much of what is frightening about works such as *Nineteen Eighty-Four* (Orwell 1949), *A Clockwork Orange* (Burgess 1962), and *Erewhon* (Butler 1872).

However, it is not only the political implications of a world without individual responsibility that strike many people as unsatisfactory. It is also that they do not recognize themselves in the descriptions given by those who deny responsibility. Consider an example from Galen Strawson (the philosopher son of Peter Strawson, whose work was discussed briefly in chapter 1):

> Suppose you set off for a shop on the evening of a national holiday, intending to buy a cake with your last £10 note. Everything is closing down. There is one cake left; it costs £10. On the steps of the shop, someone is shaking an Oxfam tin. You stop, and it seems completely clear to you that it is entirely up to you what you do next: you are truly, radically free to choose, in such a way that you will be ultimately responsible for whatever you do choose. You can put the money in the tin, or go in and buy the cake, or just walk away. You're not only completely free to choose. You are not free not to choose. (G. Strawson 1998: 747)

This kind of experience of ourselves as thinking, choosing agents gives us a sense that we are free and responsible (whatever the philosophers and scientists tell us, as it were). Yet, when we think about it – perhaps even at the time – we can be drawn towards a different set of thoughts, which revolve around the idea that what we choose to do – buy the cake or give the money to Oxfam – will be determined by the kinds of persons that we are – whether we have charitable dispositions, for example. And the kind of persons that we are is a result of our genetic inheritance and socialization. Thus, we worry that it only seems that we choose what to do, and that seeming choice cannot bring responsibility with it because it is just a reflection of the workings of genetics and environment.

Many people, when they reflect on questions of responsibility, experience the ground slipping from beneath their feet in this way. One – perhaps the main – reason for this is the advance of naturalistic explanations of both physical and social phenomena. For it seems that the more we discover about the universe, and the more we lose faith in theological accounts that set human beings apart from the rest of nature, the more it appears that we fit into the natural world just as does, and in the same way as, every other entity. We fear that what this means is that we are as subject to the determinations of the natural world as are other things. That said, the ways in which claims about the world affect claims about human freedom and responsibility are not at all clear. In the next section, various threats to responsibility are examined. The attempt is not to canvass all of them, or to review the whole of the debate over free will. Rather, the attempt is to narrow down the ways in which concerns over responsibility might matter to legal and political philosophy.

3   Threats to Responsibility

One source of anxiety about responsibility lies in the arguments for determinism. Determinism is the thesis that all events are necessitated by causes, and that the causal chain is solid. Thus, the future, like the past, is laid down for us. Or, as William James graphically put it:

> Those parts of the universe already laid down appoint and decree what other parts shall be. The future has no ambiguous possibilities hidden in its womb: the part we call the present is compatible with only one totality. Any other future complement than the one fixed from eternity is impossible. The whole is in each and every part, and welds it into the rest with an absolute unity, an iron block, in which there can be no equivocation or shadow of turning. (James 1979: 117–18)

If true, this threatens responsibility, because what happens in the world (including in human action) is the only thing that could possibly happen. It could not have been, and could not be, other than it was, is, and will be. Two steps are needed here: first, a claim about the way the world is – it is deterministic – and second, a claim that explains how the world being that way affects the idea of responsibility. One way to think about why it matters that there are two steps is to consider whether if you suddenly became convinced of the truth of determinism that, just by itself, would change your views of whether, for example, you could feel love, gratitude, or resentment towards another person, or whether you would suddenly feel that it was reasonable to think of competent adult human beings as being relevantly similar to children or non-human animals (this 'test' is discussed in Fischer 1999: 129). It should not unless and until you understand how determinism affects responsibility.

3.1   Threat 1: the absence of alternative possibilities

There is one way in which a belief in the truth of determinism seems to connect more or less directly to a common approach to responsibility. This is that if, in James's words, 'those parts of the universe already laid down appoint and decree what other parts shall be', then the future could not be other than it will be, and that violates the requirement that if someone is to be held responsible for a given action, then it must have been possible for that agent to have done other than he did (he must have been able to do otherwise). The idea is that for an agent to be morally responsible for a given action or event, then at some crucial points in his life it must have been possible for him to control which way, of at least two, he and the world would go (Fischer 1999: 99). So, we might say that Smith is responsible for getting drunk and hitting Jones only if at the time at which he got drunk he could have done otherwise, and if determinism is true, it would seem that he could not.

The alternative possibilities requirement exercises a strong hold on us. Yet, philosophy has provided a powerful counter-argument to it in the form of what are called 'Frankfurt cases' (after the philosopher Harry Frankfurt, who first developed the argument). Consider the following example (which I have slightly adapted to bring it up to date), and the conclusion that follows from it:

> Suppose Jones is in a voting booth deliberating about whether to vote for Kerry or Bush. . . . After serious reflection, he chooses to

vote for Kerry and does vote for Kerry by marking his ballot in the normal way. Unbeknownst to him, Black, a liberal neurosurgeon working with the Democratic Party, has implanted a device in Jones's brain which monitors Jones's brain activities [footnote omitted]. If he is about to choose to vote Democratic, the device simply continues monitoring and does not intervene in the process in any way. If, however, Jones is about to choose to vote (say) Republican, the device triggers an intervention which involves electronic stimulation of the brain sufficient to produce a choice to vote for the Democrat (and a subsequent Democratic vote). . . .

Given that the device plays no role in Jones's deliberations and act of voting, it seems . . . that Jones acts freely and is morally responsible for voting for Kerry. And given the presence of Black's device, it is plausible to think that Jones does not have alternative possibilities with regard to his choice and action. (Fischer 1999: 109–10; the original example referred to the 2000 election contest between Bush and Gore)

Frankfurt cases – like everything else in philosophy – are controversial,[4] but at the very least they show that it is not straightforward that responsibility requires the possibility to do otherwise, and many people are convinced that they show that responsibility definitely does not require such a possibility. Susan Hurley neatly captures the general intuition behind Frankfurt cases when she writes that it is reasonable to hold someone responsible for an action even if he could not have done otherwise if he would have done the same thing even if he had been able to do otherwise (Hurley 2003: 75). Of course, none of this is enough to show that the deterministic threat to responsibility has been thwarted. It does, however, demonstrate the complexity involved in getting from some claim or other about the way the world works to conclusions about responsibility. If determinism is true, then questions can still be asked about, for example, the role of agents in a deterministic world (we are, after all, all part of the causal story) and about responsibility. The attempt to speed through the argument by appeal to the fact that determinism precludes there being genuine alternative possibilities fails.

3.2   Threat 2: the absence of real freedom

In the example given above, the fact that Black had implanted a device in Jones's brain and so deprived Jones of the possibility of doing other than voting for Kerry seemed not to matter to our attributing responsibility to Jones for his vote, because it turned out that it was not the device, but Jones's deliberation and choice that resulted in his voting for Kerry. Had Jones changed his mind and triggered Black's device, then he would still have voted for Kerry, but we would not think him responsible, because we would say that he did not 'really' or 'genuinely' choose so to do. The device, rather than Jones himself, was the cause of his choosing Kerry. However, now a worry kicks in: if we are subject to causes – if we are not ourselves originating causes – then what distinguishes the case in which Jones votes for Kerry because he has been brought up in a liberal family, taught from an early age to be concerned with issues of social justice, and had these views reinforced throughout his education, and the case in which he votes for Kerry because Black changes his brain activities?[5] In other words, the conviction is that responsibility requires 'genuine' or 'real' choice, and the threat is that when we identify the necessary conditions for exercising such choice, they will be incompatible with what we can call, following Scanlon, 'the Causal Thesis'. This thesis is slightly weaker than the deterministic one. It states that 'all of our actions have antecedent causes to which they are linked by causal laws of the kind that govern other events in the universe, whether these laws are deterministic or merely probabilistic' (Scanlon 1998: 250).

Why might this thesis threaten the necessary conditions for 'genuine' choice? Because, we think that if it is true that all our actions result from certain causal influences – for example, our physical constitutions and the stimuli of our environments – then they are not ours in the right way – that is, 'ours' in the way that confers responsibility.

This argument is given in particularly straightforward terms by Galen Strawson, who dubs it 'the basic argument'.

Since Strawson provides a particularly clear statement of the worry, it is worth quoting in full:

> (1) It is undeniable that one is the way one is, initially, as a result of heredity and early experience, and it is undeniable that these are things for which one cannot be held to be in any way responsible (morally or otherwise). (2) One cannot in any later stage of life hope to accede to true moral responsibility for the way one is by trying to change the way one already is as a result of heredity and previous experience. For (3) both the particular way in which one is moved to try to change oneself, and the degree of one's success in one's attempt at change, will be determined by how one already is as a result of heredity and previous experience. And (4) any further changes that one can bring about only after one has brought about certain initial changes will in turn be determined, via the initial changes, by heredity and previous experience. (5) This may not be the whole story, for it may be that some changes in the way one is are traceable not to heredity and experience but to the influence of indeterministic or random factors. But it is absurd to suppose that indeterministic or random factors, for which one is ex hypothesi in no way responsible, can in themselves contribute in any way to one's being truly morally responsible for how one is.
>
> The claim, then, is not that people cannot change the way they are. They can, in certain respects (which tend to be exaggerated by North Americans and underestimated, perhaps, by Europeans). The claim is only that people cannot be supposed to change themselves in such a way as to be or become truly morally or ultimately morally responsible for the way they are, and hence for their actions. (G. Strawson 1999: 115–16)

According to Strawson, then, we begin from some position (say, birth) in which we have inherited our characteristics. We are then shaped by this inheritance and how it interacts with the environments in which we are brought up. As a result, when we choose to act – even when we choose to act on ourselves to try to change our personalities, habits, dispositions, and so on – we are moved to do this and to succeed or fail by a combination of our genetic inheritance and environment.

Since we cannot plausibly be held responsible for how we are at birth, and we cannot be responsible for the intermediate steps in our lives when our natural characteristics interact with our genetic make-ups and environments, we cannot be responsible for the latest incarnation of that interaction, in the form of our actions (addressed to ourselves, others, or the world). Indeed, who we are and what we try to do (including with ourselves) depend on other choices and circumstances that go back far beyond our births – our parents' choice to conceive on a particular occasion, their success in so doing, our mothers' choices over how to behave while pregnant, and so on – and the idea that we can be responsible for all those actions and events is absurd. There seems, then, to be nowhere for responsibility to get into the story. So, if responsibility is regressive in this way, then it is, indeed, impossible.

4   The Compatibilist Response

'Compatibilists' are so called because they believe in the truth of determinism (or of the Causal Thesis), but believe that responsibility is compatible with this truth. There are many and various (and very ingenious) compatibilist theories, and I shall briefly sketch some below, but most share a view of the kind of mistake (as they see it) made by incompatibilist philosophers like Galen Strawson. Strawson, the compatibilists allege, shows that a certain kind of human freedom is impossible: a kind that requires that human beings are originating causes of their actions. However, compatibilists claim, responsibility does not require *that* kind of freedom. Rather, it requires freedom in the sense that can be contrasted with 'coerced' rather than 'caused'.

To get a better grip on this, think back to the experience of responsibility had by the agent choosing between buying the cake and giving the £10 to Oxfam. Had the person waving the Oxfam tin put a gun to the agent's head, or had the agent been hypnotized, or were he suffering from some psychological compulsion, he would not be properly held responsible.

It is these kinds of interferences with freedom that matter, say the compatibilists, just as it matters that it is Jones's choice and not Black's device that causes Jones to vote for Kerry. It is not the fact that the agent's character was formed by things over which he had no control.

Compatibilists often pursue this general strategy, and the lead given by Peter Strawson, by examining our current practices of excusing and exempting agents from moral responsibility (a particularly good example is Wallace's *Responsibility and the Moral Sentiments* (1994)). The aim is to show that, for example, when we excuse someone for breaking into a mountain cabin during a snowstorm – an example of the excuse of duress – we do so because we think of the snowstorm as (in some sense) like having a gun to one's head. Were a different agent to break into the cabin on a sunny day and then claim, as an excuse, that his character was formed in such a way that he is predisposed to breaking and entering, we would not be impressed, but assume that (at best) he was making a bad joke (the example is taken from Barry 1997: 620). This strategy has required compatibilists to spend a great deal of time unpacking our practices of excusing and exempting both to understand and criticize those practices and to get to grips with the basic issue of what capacities an agent must have to be responsible (and the ways in which excuses and exemptions interact with those capacities).

The capacities question has proved to be particularly important and fruitful. Its importance can be gauged by returning to our agent standing outside the cake shop. This example was first presented to illustrate the experience we have of choice. Here is an agent, there are two options, so where is the problem? But, if that was all that there was to freedom and responsibility, then all kinds of things would count as free and responsible. Consider a fox confronted by an open chicken house on his left and some newly born lambs in the field on his right. Or retell the story of the agent at the cake shop specifying that she is only 9 years old. In these cases, the ordinary sense of being unconstrained holds – it would, of course, be different if the chicken house was closed or if the girl believed that her parents would kill her should she not return with a cake – but in neither case do we conclude that there is responsibility present. There must, then, be something special about adult (competent) human beings, and it should come as no surprise that what is picked out is often either self-consciousness or a capacity to act on reasons (or both).[6]

As noted above, the results of these enquiries into human capacities and our practices of excusing and exempting have been many, various, and ingenious. For present purposes, though, and at the risk of oversimplifying, it is worth looking at two broad compatibilist approaches.

4.1   Mesh compatibilists

Mesh theories are so called because they focus on 'whether there is a suitable connection or mesh between selected elements of one's mental economy' (Fischer and Ravizza 1998: 185).[7] Probably the most famous such account is owed to Harry Frankfurt.

According to Frankfurt, human beings have 'first-order desires' to do or obtain things. However, we also have second-order desires, which are desires about our (first-order) desires. Amongst these second-order desires will normally be desires about what the agent wants his will to be; that is, about which of his first-order desires he actually wants to move him to action. These Frankfurt calls 'second-order volitions'. An agent is morally responsible where there is a conformity – or mesh – between his second-order volition and his effective will. Fischer and Ravizza provide a useful gloss:

> So, for example, you may have a desire to smoke a cigarette, and a desire to refrain from smoking (for health reasons); you may then step back from these desires and form a second-order volition that your first-order preference to refrain from smoking moves you to act. Let us say that you do in fact refrain from smoking. You are morally responsible for refraining from smoking, on Frankfurt's view, insofar as there is a mesh between

your second-order volition (the preference that your desire to refrain from smoking moves you to action) and your will (the first-order desire to refrain from smoking). (Fischer and Ravizza 1998: 184)

The thought behind this theory, as behind all mesh theories (despite their differences), is a straightforward one. When a person acts, it matters to us whether that person is acting 'in character' and whether his actions genuinely express that character. Thus, to deal briefly with two variations on the theme, Gary Watson (2004) argues that a responsible agent is one in whom there is a mesh between his 'valuational preferences', which involve judgements about the worthiness of things, and his straightforwardly 'motivational preferences', which move him to act. For George Vuoso, 'an agent can properly be held morally responsible [in the sense of blamed] for his actions to the extent and only to the extent that they reflect badly on his character' (Vuoso 1987; cited in Fischer and Ravizza 1998: 186).

Mesh theories, then, adopt the following strategy in response to the threat posed by the regression requirement. Remember that threat arises because of the attention it pays to the past: if our current choices in fact arise from causes that go back far beyond our births, then it seems that those choices are not really ours in a way that could confer responsibility on us. Mesh theorists deny the importance of the past by articulating a theory of responsibility that is importantly *ahistorical.*

However, in saying that a theory of responsibility is ahistorical, we need to be careful. Fischer and Ravizza, for example, claim that mesh theories are ahistorical in the sense that they posit responsibility on the basis of a 'time-slice' or 'snapshot' of the agent's current capacities. What they mean by this is that if, for example, we consider Frankfurt's theory, whether a person is responsible or not depends on the relationship of his different-order preferences and volitions. At the time at which he acts, then, we take a snapshot of his mental economy and check in what relationship these critical elements of his mental economy stand (Fischer and Ravizza 1998: 185ff).

Now, Frankfurt may indeed believe in this kind of time-slice approach.[8] However, not all mesh theories need be like his. Consider again Vuoso's claim that 'an agent can properly be held morally responsible for his actions to the extent and only to the extent that they reflect badly on his character'. It is true that Vuoso goes on to say that 'one's past is irrelevant to the assessment of [one's] moral responsibility'; nevertheless, it is clear that character is not something easily thought of in terms of a current time-slice (see Watson 2004: 304–6). Consider an example from T. M. Scanlon:

> Suppose, for example, that someone who has previously always been kind and considerate suddenly begins making cruel and wounding remarks to her friends after being hit on the head or given drugs for some medical condition. We would not, at least at first, take this behavior as grounds for modifying our opinion of her. . . . But suppose that this behavior continues. If, after fifteen years, the person still behaves in this way and shows no signs of rejecting these attitudes or finding them 'alien' to her, then our sense of the agent being appraised is likely to shift. . . . We may say, 'She used to be so wonderful, but after her accident she became a nasty person.' (Scanlon 1998: 278–9)

Time is important in this example because 'character', like many possible contenders for being bits of our mental economy relevant to responsibility, is itself a notion that has a historical dimension; to have a certain character is to manifest certain dispositions, preferences, and so on, over time. Nevertheless, even if mesh theories do not *necessarily* have to have the kind of time-slice or snapshot nature that Fischer and Ravizza attribute to them, they remain ahistorical in an important sense. This is that responsibility consists in having some specified mesh that obtains between the relevant bits of the agent's mental economy. Even if some of those bits have a historical nature, the fact of whether the agent is or is not responsible depends on the robustly non-historical fact that the mesh does or does not obtain at the relevant moment. Shortly after the accident in the example given above, then, a mesh theorist may say that we cannot judge the responsibility of the woman for her cruelty because we cannot (temporarily) tell anything about one of the critical elements of her mental economy (we cannot judge her character). The history matters, then, but not in the sense in which it matters for Galen Strawson. Thus, even for 'character'-based mesh theorists, what matters in the end is 'what someone is like now . . . not how [his] traits were acquired' (Cummins 1980: 224). Or, in Vuoso's words, 'the sort of character a person has is relevant to assessing his moral responsibility for an action, but not how he came to have that character' (Vuoso 1987: 1681).

Galen Strawson would, of course, object. For him, history matters, and so it is wrong to say that how a person came to have a particular character is irrelevant to his moral responsibility. For Strawson, given that we have no control over how we come to have our characters, we cannot properly be held responsible for them or for the choices that arise out of them. How do we decide an issue like this? Thinking harder about the concept of responsibility is not going to do the trick. Frankfurt, Peter Strawson, and many others have thought hard about it and (whatever Galen Strawson says about its impossibility) generated complex and coherent accounts of responsibility. However, the issue is not one of conceptual coherence, but of whether these accounts of responsibility are convincing. Galen Strawson, for example, is well aware of the compatibilist position, and in replying to it he appeals to our experiences of responsibility and to what we want the idea to do. In particular, he argues that his understanding of self-determination is 'central to ordinary thought about moral responsibility and justice', and 'central to the Western religious, moral, and cultural tradition' (G. Strawson 1999: 121, 116). Or again, 'what one naturally takes oneself to be . . . is a truly self-determining agent of the impossible kind' (G. Strawson 1986: 96). That is, in defence of his central claim, Strawson raises our social practices and understandings, and argues that these only make sense against a background assumption that, to be truly morally responsible, one must be self-determining in the way that he has shown to be impossible. Compatibilist philosophers, Strawson thinks, may be able to rescue some account of responsibility that is compatible with his basic argument; but no compatibilist account could underwrite 'true moral responsibility', and so none will ever be able to secure the justice of punishments and rewards (G. Strawson 1999: 121).

However, it is clear that not everyone shares Strawson's understanding of our social practices. Brian Barry, for example, while accepting that 'people are . . . responsible for the outcomes of actions only if they are also responsible for the preferences from which those actions flow', thinks it an error to hold that, in turn, 'responsibility for preferences depends upon their being subject to choice' (Barry 1991: 156). In Robert Nozick's felicitous phrase, the foundations for desert do not themselves need to be deserved 'all the way down' (Nozick 1974: 225), and that claim appeals, too, in the case of responsibility. It seems, then, that we can trade intuitions about what really counts as responsibility and go nowhere. To avoid this, it is worth returning to the original issue raised by the examination of mesh theories.

The issue is this: mesh theorists hold that responsibility is a matter of a particular mesh obtaining at a particular time (usually, the time at which the agent acts[9]). However, if this is all that there is to it, then it would seem that the mesh could be produced in a way that we would normally think of as undermining responsibility.[10] Consider two examples.

Robert, who is genuinely undecided between two conflicting first-order desires X and Y, is visited by a hypnotist who decides to 'solve' his problem by putting him in a trance and inducing in him a second-order volition in favor of X; as a result of having this second-order volition, Robert then acts to satisfy X, never suspecting that his decisiveness has been induced by the hypnotist . . . we would all surely deny that Robert acts of his own free will, when he acts from the second-order volition induced by the hypnotist. (Slote 1980: 149; cited in Fischer and Ravizza 1998: 196)

JoJo is the favorite son of Jo the First, an evil and sadistic dictator of a small undeveloped country. Because of his father's special feelings for the boy, JoJo is given a special education and is allowed to accompany his father often and to observe his daily routine. In light of this treatment, it is not surprising that little JoJo takes his father as a role-model and develops values very much like his dad's. As an adult, he does many of the same sorts of things his father did, including sending people to prison or to death or to torture chambers on the basis of the slightest of his whims. He is not *coerced* to do these things, he acts according to his own desires. . . . In the light of JoJo's heritage and upbringing – both of which he was powerless to control – it is dubious at best that he should be regarded as responsible for what he does. (Wolf 1987: 53–4)

In both cases, it would seem that Frankfurt's mesh obtains. In the case of JoJo, it would also be the case that he acts 'in character' (and the same may be true of Robert given that X is clearly not an option alien to him). Yet, in both cases we have reason (at least) to doubt the attribution of responsibility. That is not to say that these examples are decisive – it seems to me that reasonable people may have differing intuitions about these cases – it is just to push the thought that an account of responsibility that is entirely ahistorical cannot even make space for the kinds of considerations that make us think twice when confronted by examples like these. The general form of the argument is given by Fischer and Ravizza:

The selected mesh – the relevant configuration of mental states – could . . . be produced by a wide range of intuitively 'responsibility undermining factors'. If the mesh were produced by certain sorts of brainwashing or subliminal advertising, presumably we would not hold the agent morally responsible for his behavior (in spite of the existence of the mesh). (Fischer and Ravizza 1998: 197)

4.2   *Reasons-responsiveness compatibilists*

Recall, we began by asking what difference the truth of determinism, or of the Causal Thesis, would make to responsibility.

It seemed that the difference would be in the availability of options to do otherwise, but that argument was rejected. Instead, the most significant threat was identified as coming from the regression requirement. 'Real' moral responsibility for our current actions requires that we are responsible for the causes of those actions, and for the causes of those causes, and so on. Since this requirement cannot be met, such responsibility is impossible. However, compatibilists deny that responsibility requires any such thing. Instead, one group of compatibilists – mesh compatibilists – identify responsibility as being a matter of the right mesh obtaining between various elements of agents' mental economies. The strategy is to deny the relevance of history and so defeat the threat of regression. However, by denying the importance of history, mesh theorists seem to leave out something that is important and so leave themselves vulnerable to criticisms like those offered above.

A second important group of compatibilists – reasons-responsiveness compatibilists[11] – focuses on the capacities of the agent to govern his behaviour in accordance with the demands of reasons. One strategy is to examine closely the kinds of responsibility-undermining factors (like hypnotism or brainwashing) that were important in the discussion of mesh theories. These factors, according to Wallace (who offers a reasons-responsiveness account of responsibility), operate either to *excuse* the agent – that is, to show that a generally responsible agent is not responsible for some particular act or state of affairs – or to *exempt* him from responsibility – that is, to show that the agent is not properly held responsible at all. It is worth considering this argument in a little detail.

Wallace offers a sophisticated account of responsibility building on Peter Strawson's (1962) seminal paper 'Freedom and Resentment'. His primary aim is to show that our normal practices of excusing and exempting (from moral responsibility) are underpinned by reasons that are immune to the threat posed by determinism. In other words, were determinism true, it would not be the case that the ordinary reasons we have for excusing and exempting people from responsibility would generalize to all human agents and their actions.

Following Peter Strawson, Wallace argues that holding someone responsible involves the belief that 'it would be appropriate for us to feel the reactive emotions' of 'indignation, resentment, and guilt' when that person violates moral obligations that we reasonably expect him to uphold (Wallace 1994: 62). Having thus argued for a particular account of what it is *to hold* someone morally responsible, Wallace moves to the question of what it is *to be* a morally responsible agent. The connection, Wallace argues, between holding responsible and being responsible is this: an agent is morally responsible in so far as it is fair to hold him morally responsible. What is crucial, then, is to enquire into when and why it is fair to hold someone to be morally responsible. In short, Wallace's argument is that it is fair to do so only when the person possesses the general powers 'to grasp and apply moral reasons, and to govern one's behavior by the light of such reasons' (Wallace 1994: 1). This is the sense in which he offers a 'reasons-responsiveness' compatibilism.

Wallace focuses on the areas of excusing and exempting in order to unpack our practices of holding responsible and the circumstances in which we think it (un)fair to do so. The strategy is this: there are certain conditions that we are confident make it unfair to hold people responsible in our moral practices. These conditions either excuse or exempt the agent (in the senses of these terms given above). Wallace claims, in brief, that excuses operate to show that the agent has not really done anything wrong at all, from which it follows that it would be unfair to blame him, or to feel resentful or indignant towards him. 'Excuses', as Wallace puts it, 'function not by defeating the freedom of our choices, but by indicating the absence of an ordinary choice whose content violates the moral obligations to which we are held' (Wallace 1994: 149). How does he arrive at this conclusion?

The argument depends on two critical moves: 'first, an explanation as to why the demands we hold people to should be focused on qualities of the will', and 'second, a demonstration that the full range of excuses can all be accounted for as conditions that defeat the presumption that the agent has done something morally wrong' (Wallace 1994: 119).[12] To establish the first claim, Wallace focuses on the connection between his account of responsibility and the nature of moral obligations. We blame (feel indignant or resentful towards) a person when that person has violated some moral obligation. The nature of moral obligations is that they are supported by reasons that (ideally) support and motivate people and against which we measure ourselves and others with regard to those obligations. It follows from this, according to Wallace, that '*what* one is obligated to do must be the sort of thing that could be motivated by one's grasp of the reasons expressed in moral principles' (Wallace 1994: 131). As moral reasons are practical reasons, they regulate what we do. However, it is not what we do that is directly influenced by moral reasons, but rather such reasons apply to 'bodily movements insofar as they manifest a choice that is made by the agent' (1994: 132). To give an example to illustrate the line of reasoning, someone 'who inadvertently bumps into me, thereby knocking me out of harm's way, has in no sense complied with the obligation of mutual aid' (1994: 132).

If this is right, then in the absence of some appropriate volitional element – which for the sake of brevity, let us call choice – we cannot say that someone has breached an obligation. If this is the case, then on Wallace's account of responsibility it is inappropriate to hold that person responsible, because to hold someone responsible (for example, to blame him) is to hold that he has violated a moral obligation that we accept. If excuses operate to break the link between the agent's choices and his actions, then the agent has not violated any such moral obligation and so cannot appropriately be held responsible. That is, excuses function to show that the agent has not really done anything wrong at all, and according to a settled moral conviction that we share of 'no blameworthiness without fault' (Wallace 1994: 135), that means that the agent cannot be blamed.

In short, Wallace aims to show that 'whenever people are genuinely excused from responsibility for their actions, those actions will not have been morally wrong. Obligations regulate the choices that are expressed in action, but when a valid choice obtains, it turns out that what an agent has done did not express a choice at odds with the moral obligations to which we hold that agent' (Wallace 1994: 147).

Exemptions, unlike excuses, operate to make it unfair to hold someone morally responsible at all. Building on his account that holding people to moral obligations involves committing oneself to those obligations being underpinned by (potentially) motivating reasons, Wallace argues that it can only be fair to hold those people responsible who possess two general powers of self-control: '(1) the power to grasp and apply moral reasons, and (2) the power to control or regulate [their] behavior by the light of such reasons' (Wallace 1994: 157). His defence of this claim comes in the form of a substantive principle of reasonableness: 'it is unreasonable to demand that people do something . . . if they lack the general power to grasp and comply with the reasons that support that demand' (1994: 161). Candidates for exemptions, then, include cases of 'childhood, insanity or mental illness, addiction, posthypnotic suggestion, behavior control, psychopathy, and the effects of extreme stress, deprivation, and torture' (1994: 166).[13]

Wallace's purpose, as mentioned above, is to show that our normal reasons for excusing and exempting agents would not generalize if determinism were true, and if his account of excuses and exemptions is right, then he is successful in this. As he says, the truth of determinism would not make it the case that nobody ever does anything that violates his moral obligations. Thus, if Wallace's account of excuses is right, the truth of determinism would not generalize the reasons we have for excusing people. Similarly, 'whether or not [determinism] is true would seem to have no bearing on the question of whether or not people possess the powers of reflective self-control'. The reason for this is that these 'powers are matters of broadly psychological capacity or competence, like the power to speak a given language [and] it would be very strange to suppose that determinism per se would deprive people of psychological capacities of this sort' (Wallace 1994: 181–2).

However, the threat of determinism is not the same as the threat posed by the regression requirement. We might then ask two different kinds of question about Wallace's account. First, is it right, or are there certain apparently responsibility-undermining factors for which it cannot give an adequate account? Second, even if we grant that Wallace is right, does his account provide an adequate response to Galen Strawson and the threat to responsibility created by the regression requirement?

In examining the first issue – whether Wallace's account is entirely convincing – it is worth noting that Wallace, like those who defend mesh theories, offers an entirely ahistorical account of responsibility. In excusing and exempting, according to Wallace, we should (and do) focus only on the agent's current will as manifested, or not, in his actions, and on his current capacities (or lack thereof).[14] One question that immediately comes to mind, then, is this: is Wallace's account similarly vulnerable because it ignores the importance of history? It would seem that it is. Remember that, according to Slote and Fischer and Ravizza, mesh theories are vulnerable because they cannot accommodate the fact that the relevant mesh could be the creation of some responsibility-undermining factor. Now consider the following case:

> Let us suppose that a motive, or perhaps a value, is produced in an agent via direct electronic stimulation of his brain. Imagine, for example, that a particular value, different from the agent's previous value, together with a disinclination to reflect on it in the short term, is electronically 'implanted' in an agent and that the agent performs some morally wrong act as a result. (Fischer 1996: 852)

Wallace considers cases such as this, insisting that what is critical in them is that the agent is (temporarily) disconnected from his powers of reflective self-control and so is (temporarily) a candidate for exemption:

> The imaginary cases must involve more than the mere implantation of a motive in the agent's psyche – that alone would no more

undermine responsibility than the influence of (say) television or peer pressure on the genesis of our desires. The imaginary cases must therefore be ones in which some further factor is present, and this factor seems to be that the implanted motive is supposed to lead to action in a way that (temporarily) disables the agent's ordinary powers of reflective self-control. (Wallace 1994: 197)

Two points are worth noting about this. The first is that, whatever the argument's independent merits, it does not offer a reply to the example as given. As described by Fischer, the unfortunate agent is not unable to gain access to his ordinary powers of reflection; he is simply disinclined so to do. Wallace's theory pushes him to explain the example in terms of the agent's current capacities, but the force of the example comes from the history of the agent's behaviour. This behaviour just does not seem to have the right history *vis-à-vis* the agent for it to be proper to hold him responsible for it. In this, of course, it resembles the hypnotism case that caused concern when we looked at mesh theories.

If we turn from excuses to exemptions, we see that Wallace's focus on current capacities again manifests itself in a way that threatens to render the account of exemptions less convincing. On one of the few occasions when Wallace considers the kind of example favoured by those who press regression rather than determinism in challenging responsibility, he offers the example of people raised in deprived conditions such as circumstances of 'physical and verbal abuse, emotional neglect and inattention . . . extreme arbitrariness and hypocrisy in the application of punishments and rewards, and an atmosphere of violence, insecurity, and hopelessness' (Wallace 1994: 232). As Wallace notes, the problem here is not one born of determinism. We do not need to think that everyone brought up in any of these circumstances will necessarily turn out bad. Rather, we worry that it may be *unfair* to hold someone brought up in these circumstances fully morally responsible should he turn out bad.

However, Wallace's focus on the agent's current choices and capacities means that he can only explain our reaction to the deprived wrongdoer in terms of the wrongdoer's reduced capacities for reflective self-control. Thus, he writes:

> It is extremely plausible to suppose that how far one's powers of reflective self-control are developed will largely be a function of the environmental and educational circumstances to which one is exposed in childhood and youth. If this is correct, then we can begin to understand the sensitivity of our judgments of responsibility to facts about childhood deprivation. . . . People exposed to [deprived] conditions will often find it extremely difficult to take moral requirements seriously as independent constraints on what they do. . . . On this account of it, childhood deprivation affects the adult's responsibility only insofar as it leaves continuing traces in the adult's psychological life. (Wallace 1994: 232–3)

The last of these claims is surely right. As Wallace says, it would be 'paradoxical' to think that childhood deprivation mattered to our current assessment of the resulting adult unless that deprivation had *some* continuing effect on the adult. The question is, 'What continuing effect?' For Wallace, the continuing effect is one of impairing or disabling the agent's normal powers of reflective self-control. Now, of course, it is important to grant that Wallace is right in thinking that environmental and educational circumstances may well impair the development of the powers of reflective self-control, and that an agent who lacks such powers ought not to be held responsible. The trouble is that this is the *only* way in which Wallace can accommodate a history of deprivation. Yet, in many cases what troubles us is *not* that the agent lacks a current capacity for reflective self-control, but that his capacities are informed by twisted values acquired in childhood.

Think again of the example of JoJo given above. What troubles us about the story of JoJo is surely what Strawson alleges should trouble us (although not necessarily in the way Strawson would allege): the adult JoJo is the product of his background. Given the way he was brought up, we worry that it would be unfair to hold him fully responsible for his later evil deeds. However, when we think about why it is that we worry that it might be unfair to hold him responsible, it is not because we think that he now lacks a *capacity* to control his behaviour in accordance with reasons, it is because he responds to twisted reasons. Even if one is not convinced that it would be unfair to hold JoJo responsible – perhaps one thinks that JoJo is fully responsible – the fact that the story of JoJo makes us stop and think should also give us reason to pause before adopting Wallace's account. For Wallace offers us no space at all for thinking that the details of JoJo's history themselves matter when thinking about his responsibility.[15]

In short, Wallace's account strains our ordinary moral experience in treating our responses to deprived wrongdoers as *necessarily* responses to a current lack of the powers of reflective self-control. The alternative is to think that at least some deprived wrongdoers have these powers, but that their pasts have inculcated the 'wrong' values in them.[16] Not only is this more plausible for at least some deprived wrongdoers, but it is an account that does not have the somewhat unpalatable consequence (as Wallace's does) of treating deprived wrongdoers as not really agents at all, but rather as something analogous to children or dangerous animals.

Wallace's account of both excuses and exemptions, then, is vulnerable to worries similar to those that arose when we looked at mesh theories. In offering a rigorously ahistorical account, Wallace is unable to account for some responsibility-undermining factors. However, it is worth asking the second of the questions posed above. Even if we were to grant that Wallace's account is right, would it answer the threat posed by the regression requirement? If Wallace is right, then he has successfully shown that it is not the need for regressive actual control – and its impossibility – that underwrites our practices of excusing and exempting. However, supporters of Galen Strawson might simply say that all this shows is that our current practices of excusing and exempting ought to be revised. Moreover, they can say this not on the basis of a conceptual or metaphysical claim that only things that are *causa sui* could be responsible. Rather, supporters of the regression requirement can take up Wallace's challenge to find an alternative principle of fairness to those he offers (or, perhaps, an alternative interpretation of them). As we have seen, the principles to which Wallace appeals are 'no blameworthiness without (i) fault and (ii) the capacity to comply'. The principle that inspires the regressive worry, when combined with what we know about ourselves, is 'no blameworthiness for bad luck'. That, according to Strawson and many others, goes at least as deep with us as do the principles offered by Wallace.

Before moving on to a different reasons-responsiveness account – one that explicitly includes a historical dimension in order to respond to the kinds of worries we have been discussing – it is worth pausing to ask whether the examples and arguments given above about history either beg the question, by assuming the importance of history, or lend unqualified support to Strawson's argument. Take these in reverse order. The examples of hypnotism, neurological intervention, and upbringing might be thought to lend support to Strawson's allegation that moral responsibility is impossible given that they appeal to the history of the agent's desires and motivations and to his lack of control over that history. However, one should not be too quick in assuming that thinking about these examples leads unproblematically to Strawson's position. In each case, the *details* of the stories matter. Indeed, were we to be asked to think more about to what degree, if at all, we want to hold JoJo, or the hypnotized or manipulated agent, responsible, there is (I think) every chance that we would want to know more. We might, for example, want to know exactly to what degree JoJo was kept away from other values, perhaps what education he had apart from that given to him by his father, and so on. But, if Strawson is right, these details do not matter. Indeed, the stories need have no details whatsoever. JoJo and the hypnotized and the manipulated agents are not each *causa sui* because no human being could be the cause of itself. Their stories, it is true, are more dramatic than most, but the past matters to Strawson just because we all have one. The content of our particular histories is irrelevant. Yet, invoking these examples against ahistorical theories like Frankfurt's and Wallace's does not have to give rise to *that* thought. Indeed, for most people making judgements about responsibility, the precise details of the stories matter enormously.

For related reasons it is hard to reply to the allegation that to take history seriously is to beg the question. There is one sense in which this charge is right. Accounts of responsibility must, in the end, be tested against our experiences of holding people responsible, and this inevitably involves testing them against examples. People may have different intuitions and responses to these examples, and at the limit, there is perhaps nothing that can be done where these responses differ dramatically. Thus, if someone finds that JoJo's story or the stories of hypnotism and brain manipulation make no difference to his intuitions about responsibility, there is probably little that can be done to convince him that responsibility has a historical dimension. In short, these examples are supposed to show that there is a strong intuitive sense that certain kinds of histories are responsibility-undermining. If someone disagrees, then very little of the rest of this book (or of what he has read so far) will appeal to him. However, this is *not* to beg the question by assuming what Strawson set out to show – that moral responsibility is impossible – for precisely the reason given above. All that has been argued is that history matters; nothing has been said about the precise way in which it matters. Indeed, as noted above, in so far as these examples suggest ways in which history matters, they do so in the profoundly un-Strawsonian way of making the details matter.

Many of the arguments concerning the importance of history and the failure of mesh theories and Wallace's account are stressed by Fischer and Ravizza in various pieces of work. Fischer and Ravizza's positive theory is itself a reasons-responsiveness one, and the second theory of that kind we will examine here, but (as one would expect given their criticisms of others) one that they believe properly captures the significance of history.

Fischer and Ravizza, like Wallace, follow the lead given by Peter Strawson in holding that

Someone is morally responsible insofar as he is an appropriate candidate for the reactive attitudes. More specifically, someone is a morally responsible *agent* insofar as he is an appropriate candidate for at least some of the reactive attitudes on the basis of at least some of his behavior (or perhaps his character). And someone is morally responsible *for a particular bit of behavior* (or perhaps a trait of character) to the extent that he is an appropriate candidate for at least some of the reactive attitudes on the basis of that behavior (or trait of character). (Fischer and Ravizza 1998: 6–7)

Of course, as with Wallace, what are critical are the conditions under which someone is an appropriate candidate for the reactive attitudes. Fischer and Ravizza hold that appropriate candidates must meet two kinds of conditions: 'epistemic' and 'freedom-relevant' (1998: 13). The intuition in the case of the 'epistemic condition' they attribute to Aristotle. It is that to be appropriately held responsible, one should not be 'deceived or ignorant' about what one is doing or about the consequences of one's actions (unless one is culpable for one's ignorance) (1998: 12–13).

The focus of Fischer and Ravizza's book is the 'freedom-relevant condition', which they also refer to as the 'control condition' because it stipulates that 'an agent must *control* his behavior in a suitable sense, in order to be morally responsible for it' (1998: 13). Fischer and Ravizza are convinced that responsibility does not require alternative possibilities, because they are convinced by Frankfurt's arguments (discussed above) (1998: 29f). Thus, they do not believe that the kind of control a responsible agent need have requires the availability of alternative possibilities. Rather, they argue that what is needed is what they call 'guidance control' (1998: 31).

What exactly is 'guidance control'? It requires that 'in order to be morally responsible for an action, the agent must act from a mechanism that is his own reasons-responsive mechanism' (Fischer and Ravizza 1998: 81). This formula contains two elements: 'a reasons-responsive mechanism' and the requirement that that mechanism be 'the agent's own'. Take these in turn.

What it is for an agent to act from a reasons-responsive mechanism is complex, and as Robert Kane put it in a review of Fischer and Ravizza's book, 'it is best to explain this formula by example': 'Suppose Sally chooses to make a right turn at the traffic lights. In making this choice, she is (moderately) "reasons-responsive" if, were she to have had a sufficient reason to do otherwise (e.g., to choose to turn left), she would have recognized that reason, and might have acted for it and thus chosen otherwise.' In order to explain how this kind of control does not require alternative possibilities, Kane continues:

> Now it turns out that if a Frankfurt controller were present, her choice would not have been 'reasons-responsive' in this way, because the controller would have prevented her from choosing otherwise even if she had had a sufficient reason to do so. That is why Fischer and Ravizza opt for what they call a 'mechanism-based' approach to moral responsibility as opposed to an agent-based approach (Fischer and Ravizza 1998: 38). Though Sally cannot do otherwise, given the presence of the controller, if she chooses to turn right on her own then her choice issues from a reasons-responsive *mechanism* (e.g., a deliberative process) that is her own, and so she is still responsible for it. While she lacks regulative control (the power to do otherwise), she none the less has guidance control: her act issues from 'a moderately reasons-responsive mechanism' that is her own. (Kane 1999: 543–4, adapting an example taken from Fischer and Ravizza 1998: 32)

The thought here is familiar from the earlier discussion of Frankfurt cases. So long as Sally deliberated properly and the decision to turn resulted in the right kind of way from that deliberation, then it seems appropriate to hold her responsible whether or not she could have done otherwise. However, this, as we have seen, is not the most pressing threat to responsibility. Rather, the greatest danger comes from the regression requirement. This concerns not the specification of the reasons-responsive mechanism, but rather the requirement that the mechanism be *the agent's own*. As we have seen, Fischer and Ravizza themselves are very concerned by this, and they criticize Wallace, whose account is otherwise similar to their own, for ignoring the importance of history.

Of course, Fischer and Ravizza are aware that a mechanism cannot be the agent's own in the *causa sui* sense favoured by Galen Strawson. Sally's past, the preferences she has inherited, and numerous other things over which she has had no control, undoubtedly led to her being at a particular intersection at a particular time and wishing, after deliberation, to turn one way rather than another. She does not exercise some radically free ungrounded choice at the moment she reaches the crossroads. What, then, do they mean by saying that a reasons-responsive mechanism must be the agent's own?

Fischer and Ravizza offer an extended discussion of the 'agent's own' element of the control condition. They conclude that an action is the agent's own if he 'takes responsibility' for it.[17] This involves 'three major ingredients':

1 'An individual must see himself as the source of his behavior in the sense that . . . the individual must see himself as an agent; he must see that his choices and actions are efficacious in the world. The agent thus sees that his motivational states are the causal source – in certain characteristic ways – of upshots in the world.'
2 'The individual must accept that he is a fair target of the reactive attitudes as a result of how he exercises this agency in certain contexts.'
3 'The individual's view of himself specified in the first two conditions be based, in an appropriate way, on the evidence.' (All quotations are from Fischer and Ravizza 1998: 210–13)

The idea is to use these three ingredients to exclude the kinds of examples that Fischer and Ravizza believe undermine Wallace's account (and all ahistorical accounts). Remember, then, Fischer's example of someone who performs a wrong act as a result of a motive that is produced in him via direct electronic stimulation of his brain (Fischer 1996: 852, discussed above). In such a case, if the agent were aware of the intervention, he would not meet condition (2).

That is, he might agree that it was his motivational state that was the causal source (remember, he has a motive implanted in him), but given that the source of his motivational state was, say, a neurosurgeon who implanted the motive, he would not accept that he is a fair target for the reactive attitudes. Thus, he might say, 'Okay, I did it, but if you are going to blame anyone, blame the neurosurgeon,' and we would surely agree. He might, of course, deny that he meets condition (1) and claim that although he was the carrier of the motivational state, it was the neurosurgeon's and not *his* motivational state that was the causal source of the act. If so, he fails to meet both conditions (1) and (2). Either way, it seems that the 'taking responsibility' model can cope with this example as specified.

However, what if the agent is not aware of the intervention? If we drop this part of the story, and substitute that the neurosurgeon implants the motive in a way that ensures that the agent will believe the motive to be his own, then Fischer and Ravizza admit that the agent will meet conditions (1) and (2) (1998: 235–6). He will think of himself as an agent, acting on his own motives, and as an apt recipient of the reactive attitudes that arise from his action. Given that Fischer and Ravizza (and most people) would not think this person responsible (if anything, this intuition is stronger in the case where the manipulated agent does not know that he is being manipulated), it is condition (3) that is going to have to do the work. This condition requires that the agent's view of his motives as the causal source of the action (his recognition of (1)), and his acceptance of it being apt to hold him subject to the reactive attitudes (2), are based '*in an appropriate way*, on the evidence' (emphasis added). Thus, Fischer and Ravizza write of condition (3) that it 'is intended (in part) to imply that an individual who has been electronically induced to have the relevant view of himself (and thus satisfy the first two conditions on taking responsibility) has *not* formed his view of himself in the appropriate way' (1998: 236).

How does this condition achieve this? What is it to view oneself in the appropriate way? Unfortunately, Fischer and

Ravizza conclude the passage just quoted with the remark 'but the relevant notion of appropriateness must remain unanalyzed' (1998: 236). What seems right about this (as it has all along) is that Fischer and Ravizza wish to include a historical element in their account. The problem is that, as we have seen, the precise way in which history matters is what matters. And to leave 'appropriateness' unanalysed thus leaves the account without a critical element. In so doing, it invites incompatibilists (those who deny that responsibility and determinism can be compatible) and others to turn the kinds of issues that Fischer and Ravizza deployed against Wallace back against them. Consider the following from Robert Kane:

> In order to rule out freedom-undermining conditions such as brainwashing, behavioural engineering and the like, I think the 'appropriateness' of evidence must imply that the agents are not *in fact* covertly controlled, no matter what they believe. And if this is so, there is a problem here . . . . If a mechanism, such as a deliberative process, is not 'the agent's own' when its operation and outcomes are determined by a team of behavioural engineers operating covertly . . . how then is it the agent's own if it is produced by normal conditioning procedures of upbringing and society . . ., if *those* procedures of social conditioning are also covertly determining to the same effect? Is the difference that the behavioural engineers know what they are doing and society does not? But what is the difference for my freedom and responsibility if I am controlled by dumb controllers rather than smart ones, if the control in either case is complete? (Kane 1999: 544–5)

Think again of JoJo, whose upbringing is unusual in its content (he is the son of a dictator and spends his time visiting prisons, etc.), but not in the way in which it is done (JoJo is not brainwashed or hypnotized; he is just raised by an attentive father whom he wishes to emulate). Whether or not JoJo is appropriately held responsible, Kane's question forces us to think about what distinguishes JoJo (and so the rest of us) from the agent whose character and actions are determined by a team of behavioural engineers? Wallace, as we have seen, would opt to distinguish JoJo from the rest of us by speculating that JoJo lacked some current capacity, but Fischer and Ravizza criticize this move, emphasizing that history matters in a way that Wallace fails to capture. The problem is that if history matters, it is hard to see why Fischer and Ravizza's objections to both mesh compatibilists and Wallace do not apply to their theory, too.

It is important to distinguish two arguments here. One is the kind of argument appealed to by Galen Strawson, a version of which Fischer and Ravizza firmly reject. They consider what they call 'the transfer principle', which requires that moral responsibility can be transferred *only* from states for which the person was also morally responsible (that is, it is a version of Strawson's regression requirement). This they reject (Fischer and Ravizza 1998: ch. 6). By appealing to history, then, they want to appeal to less than transfer, but to more than the idea that history simply explains how a person got to have the current capacities (or lack thereof) that he has. This intermediate position focuses, as we have seen, on the current mechanism that gives rise to the action – and whether that mechanism is reasons-responsive – but is concerned, too, with *how* that mechanism came to be in place (Fischer and Ravizza 1998: 230–1). Condition (3) is meant to rule out the mechanism arising from responsibility-undermining factors, but it is unclear that it can do this successfully.

Put crudely, the problem is this: remember that when replying to an example in which a motive was implanted in an agent's psyche, Wallace commented that we needed to know more about its current effect because otherwise it would be impossible to distinguish this case (which is clearly meant to make us think that the agent is not responsible) from the influence of 'television or peer pressure' (Wallace, cited above). Galen Strawson, of course, would agree on the basis that there really is no difference, since the things that constitute us (whether our mother's choice to conceive, or television, or peer pressure) are such that none of us can be *causa sui*, and so none of us can be responsible. Fischer and Ravizza reject that argument, but they also reject Wallace's approach. For Fischer and Ravizza a certain kind of television

– one that involves subliminal advertising – may well be responsibility-undermining. Their difficulty is to distinguish those cases in which the way in which the reasons-responsive mechanism came to be in place undermines responsibility from cases in which it does not. The idea of 'taking responsibility' is meant to do that, but its under-analysed nature leaves us with little more than our intuitions, and those, as we have seen, are a very unreliable and inconsistent guide.

5   Going Around in Circles

In a general survey of the issue of responsibility, Galen Strawson comments that 'the problem of free will is like a carousel', because one starts with compatibilism, but soon finds that no compatibilist argument can satisfy one's intuitions about moral responsibility. However, the denial of determinism leaves us equally unsatisfied, since it leaves our actions in the grip of random or indeterministic occurrences. So it seems that the kind of 'ultimate' or 'true' moral responsibility that we seek is impossible. Thus, we return to the compatibilist position, which holds out the hope of saving some kind of responsibility, but this fails to satisfy our intuitions about responsibility, and so on (G. Strawson 1998: 753). Strawson concludes with a remark of André Gide's: 'Everything has been said before, but since nobody listens we have to keep going back and beginning all over again.' Given the discussion above, it is rather hard to avoid Strawson's rather depressing conclusion. Each of the positions examined seems to have something going for it – acting in character and the capacity to respond to reasons surely do matter to responsibility – yet the threat of the regression requirement – the need to take history seriously – undermines our confidence in these positions. Yet, as Strawson predicts, this returns us to the thought that if responsibility is regressive, then it is impossible, and that, too, is unsatisfactory.

Rather than take another turn on the carousel, we might follow an alternative approach and stop looking for answers by further analysis of the concept of responsibility and instead ask what function the idea of responsibility serves in our various practices. Of course, those influenced by Peter Strawson – like Wallace and Fischer and Ravizza – do take seriously our practices of holding responsible (the place of the reactive attitudes in our lives), but they do so, nevertheless, in pursuit of the idea of responsibility and of a resolution to the metaphysical issue of whether responsibility can be compatible with determinism. Bernard Williams, by contrast, thinks that the best way to approach the problem of responsibility is by stopping thinking of it as a problem and instead focusing only on what we do with it.

In his book *Shame and Necessity*, Williams (1993) identifies four 'basic elements of any conception of responsibility'. These are 'cause, intention, state, and response': 'that in virtue of what he did, someone has brought about a bad state of affairs; that he did or did not intend that state of affairs; that he was or was not in a normal state of mind when he brought it about; and that it is his business, if anyone's, to make up for it' (Williams 1993: 55).

Although these are 'universal materials', Williams claims that 'there is not, and there never could be, just one appropriate way of adjusting these elements to one another', and thus there is no 'one correct conception of responsibility', and he warns against the hubristic supposition that 'we have evolved a definitely just and appropriate way' of combining these materials, which we label 'moral responsibility' (Williams 1993: 55–6).

If Williams is right, then this suggests an even deeper contextualization of the notion of responsibility than is indicated by Wallace and others influenced by Peter Strawson. In fact, the notion of responsibility becomes, on Williams's account, almost insignificant as an object of study, since its content will be given by what we want it to do. Thus, he says of the contrast between ancient Greek and modern understandings of criminal responsibility that they arise 'because we [moderns] have a different view [from the Greeks], not of responsibility in general, but of the role of the state in ascribing responsibility, in demanding a response for certain acts and certain harms' (Williams 1993: 65). This does not mean that responsibility is nothing but a social construct that could take any form, or pick out any set of facts, whatsoever. It must, if it is to be a conception of responsibility at all, revolve around the four basic elements of cause, intention, state, and response.

This is a significant constraint. The social and legal practices in a given territory could not, for example, determine responsibility on grounds of hair colour (say, all and only red-headed people are responsible); holding responsible, for a given event or state, the red-headed person (geographically) closest to the occurrence of that event or state even where the person was not involved in bringing about that event or state. For this would be to ignore the primary element of cause.[18] None the less, even given this constraint, the question of how many conceptions of responsibility might properly arise remains fairly open. Not only can the four elements be combined in different ways, but each can be weighted differently. And in deciding how to combine them and with what weighting, our attention should be directed *not* at trying to get it right (to get, as it were, to the correct understanding, or meaning, of responsibility), but at what we want to do with the notion and at the context in which it operates.

Williams's argument makes some philosophers irate (and it seems to me that it attracts very little attention in the literature on responsibility). However, it may be that this is in part a reaction to the particular expression that Williams gives to his thesis. For much of the chapter in which he deals with responsibility, Williams focuses on the example of Oedipus. Oedipus, of course, killed his father Laius and married his mother, Iocasta. Concentrate only on the killing of Laius and the charge of parricide. Oedipus does not know that the man he kills is Laius, and so his actions do not give expression to a parricidal will. He is a candidate to be excused (of this charge if not of killing an old man). Yet, Williams argues that the fact that it was Oedipus who killed his father matters, for 'we know that in the story of one's life there is an authority exercised by what one has done, and not merely by what one has intentionally done' (Williams 1993: 69). Oedipus is, in important ways, held responsible by the Chorus (and the citizens of Thebes), and he holds himself responsible (as is manifested in his blinding himself).

Towards the end of the chapter, Williams pushes even harder when dealing with the story of Ajax. Ajax is made temporarily mad by Athene, and thinking that he is battling Odysseus and his enemies, he slaughters a flock of sheep.[19] On regaining his sanity, he commits suicide because he is unable to live with what he has done (having been made to look a fool). Williams wants the reader to understand Ajax – even if we would now react differently to such a situation – and, in understanding Ajax, to see that the Greeks understood something important: that 'the responsibilities we have to recognise extend in many ways beyond our normal purposes and what we intentionally do' (1993: 74).

It is this kind of thing that has the potential to enrage contemporary philosophers. Ajax, after all, is made mad by a goddess, and to treat him as responsible for his actions fits ill with our understanding of the concept. However, one needs to be extremely careful in interpreting Williams. He is not, after all, alleging that Ajax 'really was' responsible in some metaphysical sense that the Greeks understood and we moderns have lost. Far from it. Williams is clear that another person would not have to respond as Ajax responded. Indeed, he entertains the idea (suggested, he says, in Euripides' *The Madness of Heracles*) that even Ajax did not have to respond as he did (1993: 73–4). All – although it is a great deal – that Williams is urging is a displacing of the centrality of intention (or voluntariness) from our understanding of responsibility. Williams alleges that we think that if only we could pin down the notion of intentional, voluntary action, then all else with respect to a theory of responsibility would fall into place. For Williams, this approach is built upon, and conceals, two errors: first, the belief that notions like intentionality and voluntariness can be deepened very much,[20] and second, the supposition that 'public practices of ascribing responsibility can be derived from an antecedent notion of moral responsibility, or that the idea of the voluntary is uniquely important to responsibility' (1993: 67–8).

5.1   *Williams and Wallace on responsibility and regression*

It is worth pausing to ask where this leaves us, and to do so by briefly comparing Wallace and Williams on the two cases in hand. For Wallace, 'to do something of kind x, one must believe that what one is undertaking to do is of kind x, at the time that one makes the choice to do it' (1994: 136). Oedipus did not believe that what he was undertaking was parricide at the time he chose to do it, so (on this charge) Oedipus is excused. Ajax is (temporarily) mad, and thus lacks the capacity to comply with his obligations, and so is exempt from responsibility.

It is much more difficult to give the same kind of summary on behalf of Williams. He might say of Oedipus that on a *criminal* charge of parricide, Oedipus is not properly held responsible. However, it is essential to grasp that were this what he would say, it would be because of a conception of the law and not because of a general conception of responsibility. This is in stark contrast to Wallace, who writes in relation to excuses that, as a conceptual matter, 'if s did not do x intentionally, then there is a clear sense in which there is no action that s performed at all; precisely because s did not do x intentionally, we may conclude that x was not really something that s *did*' (Wallace 1994: 123–4).

Williams could hardly disagree more. As he says of Oedipus, 'the whole of the *Oedipus Tyrannus*, that dreadful machine, moves to the discovery of just one thing, that *he did it*' (1993: 69). How we, and he, should understand what he did, and what the appropriate response is to what he did, is a complex matter that depends, in part, on perspective and context. However, that Oedipus did it, and that (at least in some contexts) that he did it matters, is for Williams (as, indeed, for Oedipus) beyond question.

Williams says less about the case of Ajax. And, again, in reconstructing what he might have said, one has to pay attention to the context. To a greater degree than in the case of Oedipus, it would seem unlikely – given the purposes and functions of the criminal law (now, or in ancient Greece) – that Ajax would properly be held criminally liable for his acts. Given other purposes and functions, and, most importantly, given Ajax's self-understanding and his understanding of the roles played by people like him (of whom, of course, there are very few), his taking responsibility, in the sense of realizing that these were his acts, is understandable and proper. As Williams puts it, 'being what he is, he could not live as the man who had done these things; it would be merely impossible, in virtue of the relations between what he expects of the world and what the world expects of a man who expects that of it' (1993: 73).

5.2 Virtuous or vicious circles?

Wallace's and Williams's accounts of responsibility, then, give rise to very different judgements in the two cases of Oedipus and Ajax. Both theorists believe that responsibility is best approached by looking at the context in which judgements of responsibility are made – the practices of holding responsible – but Williams offers more pluralistic possibilities because, in the end, he thinks that there is no one right way of conceiving of responsibility to be found within these practices. Such a view may well offend our modern, progressivist tendencies. Of course, we might say, we can *understand* the regret that Oedipus and Ajax feel. We might even believe that there would be something slightly odd, and none too admirable, about a person who in a similar situation lived out his life untroubled by what he had done. However, the truth in both cases is that they were not responsible for their actions and they are not candidates for blame. That we understand this, and that the Greeks did not, is evidence of the progress that we have made in our understanding of the world and in the ways in which we conceive of our relations one to another.

This view seems to be committed to something like the following claims: that understanding the concept of responsibility may require that we attend to the context in which it is used, but that it is not entirely contextual, for there is a core notion of responsibility to be uncovered; that core notion includes the elements that Williams mentions – cause, intention, state, and response – but primary amongst these is intention (which we understand as connected to voluntariness); our understanding of intentionality is better than the understandings of the past, in part because we know more about the world (including about human psychology and the human brain) and how it works; finally, our understanding of political, moral, and social relations is better – and, in particular, more humane – than the understandings of the past, in part because we have cleansed them of beliefs that made sense only against a background of other beliefs about the world, which were mistaken (such as religious beliefs and quasi-biological beliefs such as that some people are natural slaves).

Given Williams's views on the natural sciences, he may accept some of these claims to progress, but these are the claims that relate to mistakes about, for example, causality. So, a society that, having suffered from a bad harvest, thought itself collectively responsible because its sinning ways had offended God, or thought that witches were responsible, would be mistaken. Sinning and witches do not cause bad harvests. Moreover, it is plausible to think that our understanding of notions such as intention and voluntariness has advanced with progress in the natural sciences. However, these are issues that come within Williams's four core elements. The problems come with the other claims. For example, that our conception of responsibility is better and more humane. This is an easy belief to have: our reaction to Ajax will strike us as right (but then it would). If Williams is right, though, the fact that we respond differently from the ancient Greeks does not tell us anything about the concept of responsibility; it tells us about ourselves and, to a lesser extent, about the ancient Greeks. Remember, Williams's claim about the four basic elements of responsibility is a strong one: 'there is not, *and there never could be*, just one appropriate way of adjusting these elements to one another . . . just one correct conception of responsibility' (1993: 55, emphasis added).

This stance makes it impossible to give a Williamsite response to the regression requirement. Nevertheless, Williams can be co-opted to the cause of opposing Galen Strawson's argument for the impossibility of responsibility, because if there is no one correct conception of responsibility, then there is no space for regression to make responsibility impossible. It may be that there are certain contexts in which the regression requirement is important, but if so, that is because of the contexts (the purposes of, for example, the criminal law or the institutions of distributive justice), *not* because of some discovery about what constitutes responsibility proper. If Williams is right, then, things get both much more simple and much more difficult. They get more simple, because seemingly interminable debates about free will or about what it is to act voluntarily dissolve. As Williams remarks, 'just as there is a "problem of evil" only for those who expect the world to be good, there is a problem of free will only for those who think that the notion of the voluntary can be metaphysically deepened' (1993: 68). However, things get more difficult, because in order to get at the idea of responsibility – with a view to understanding or revising it – in any given context, one has to unpack the context. For example, in order to understand the idea of responsibility as it operates in the criminal law, we need to think about the purposes of the criminal law, and this, in turn, means that we need to think about the relationships of the State to the citizen and of citizens one to another.[21] The question at the heart of this chapter, 'Is responsibility regressive?', thus fractures into lots of questions – 'Is responsibility regressive in the criminal law?', 'and/or in tort law?', 'and/or in our personal relationships, including with ourselves?', 'and/or in the moral case?', and so on – each of which requires separate examination of the purposes and demands that we make of the criminal law, tort law, personal relationships, and morality.

This fracturing of the question of responsibility is really what separates Williams from other Peter Strawson-inspired philosophers. At the limit, the idea of responsibility is determined, within the loose constraints of involving the four core elements, by the context in which it is used. If so, responsibility could mean very different things in different contexts.

Interestingly, just such a position is foreshadowed in the discussion of madness and crime in chapter 19 of James Fitzjames Stephen's *History of the Criminal Law of England* (1883). Stephen constructs the chapter as a clash between 'the medical and the legal professions'. The former are said to ascribe 'cruelty, ignorance, prejudice, and the like' to the law on the grounds that the law has failed to keep pace with discoveries in the area of mental health and illness (1883: 124–5). Stephen's reply on behalf of the law, as glossed by Hart, is that 'the doctors . . . were attempting illicitly to thrust upon juries their views on what should excuse a man when charged with a crime: illicitly, because responsibility is a matter not of science but of law' (Hart 1965: 9). Williams might well say that responsibility 'is a different matter in science and in law', but the shape of the argument is similar. For both, the progressive forces of those who think that they have discovered the truth about (in)voluntary action and responsibility are making a kind of category mistake.

The trouble with this, though, is that it leaves us in the dark about two critical issues: how should we go about examining and criticizing our understandings of responsibility? And, relatedly, how should we choose between two rival accounts of responsibility (within a particular practice)? The first question contains within it a subsidiary question, which is: How are different understandings of responsibility from within different contexts related? Only by answering these questions will it be possible to see whether the circular form of enquiry recommended by Williams is virtuous or vicious.

These methodological worries arise because of the inherent conservatism of the position that Williams stakes out. Critical reflection on responsibility comes to resemble what, in a different context, Michael Walzer calls 'social criticism'

(Walzer 1987, 1988): that is, the unpacking of meanings from within practices. Of course, unpacking meanings can, as Walzer insists it must, have a critical dimension. For example, in the criminal law, we may argue over whether strict liability offences are consistent with the conception of responsibility that we favour given the purposes of the criminal law.

Consider three positions that might emerge from a discussion of strict liability, responsibility, and the purposes of the law.

(a)   Strict liability offences do not appeal to a different conception of responsibility from that appealed to in the rest of the criminal law; they just move the point at which responsibility is attributed one step back (for example, we ascribe responsibility for an agent getting into the business of selling milk knowing that that business comes with the risk of being held liable for an employee selling contaminated milk).

(b)   The purposes of the criminal law are both forward-looking (to influence people's future behaviour) and backward-looking (to censure people for past wrongdoing). The conception of responsibility appealed to varies with these purposes. Strict liability offences are designed to make people – for example, those who are in the milk business – vigilant and careful, given the public importance of the jobs that they are doing. Thus, strict liability rules are justified in straightforward utilitarian terms, and ought to be thought of only in these terms. This means that they appeal to a fundamentally different idea of responsibility from that appealed to in other offences, and it is sophistry to pretend otherwise. Because of this, strict liability offences ought to be limited to relatively minor offences, and ought to be used sparingly.

(c)   What is said about strict liability offences in (b) is true, but the argument ought to go further. Our belief in the retributivist function of the criminal law is deeply embedded, but it cannot be defended. We should, therefore, revise our legal practices and stop pretending that the (whole of the) law is anything other than a clumsy mechanism for influencing future behaviour. All offences should be treated as strict liability offences, since the only purpose of the criminal law is to find out who did what so that offenders can be handed over to those who will incapacitate where necessary and reform them where possible.

Similar positions could be mapped out covering various controversies that rage in the law. The troubling issue is: How are we to choose between them? The tests of coherence and consistency, which might be thought to provide a starting point for reflection, may themselves be contested. For example, proponents of (a) and (c) might allege that position (b) is inadequate, because the law as a whole must appeal to one conception of responsibility. However, that is a substantive point and one that proponents of (b) will resist. Similarly, proponents of (c) might argue that it is incoherent to allow developments in our understanding of responsibility in one realm – say, in mental health and psychiatry – to go unnoticed in other realms such as the criminal law. It brings the law into disrepute, they might argue, if it continues to maintain an understanding of responsibility that is thought to be outdated in other professional fields. This, of course, is what Stephen's 'men of medicine' allege against his 'men of law', and it is a position that Stephen robustly rejects.

Resolving the debate between (a), (b), and (c), then, requires that we move the argument to the level of the purposes of the criminal law, and that means moving the argument all the way up to the most basic questions of political philosophy and practice: questions concerning the proper relations between the State and its citizens and between the citizens one to another. It is clear that this is what Williams has in mind. Writing of 'progressivist critics of the ancient world', Williams remarks that they 'sometimes give the impression of thinking that modern penology makes rational sense'. He continues, 'but whether they have that strange belief is beside the point. The point is that the question whether this part, or any other, of the legal system is in good shape or not can be discussed only in terms of what we demand of a legal system, and of how we conceive the powers of the state' (Williams 1993: 65).

If this is right, then enquiries into responsibility in almost any area will require enormous interpretive effort across many dimensions of human life. This gives rise to three concerns. First, we might wonder whether there is any way of keeping the enquiry manageable, for it seems that every enquiry into an issue of responsibility will require us to go all the way to the proper relations that ought to hold between agents and between agents and the State. Second, the idea that different demands made by different contexts will give rise to different conceptions of responsibility may put enormous strain on our practices. If in one area of our lives we (whether rightly or wrongly) are more and more taken by the significance of naturalism and the insignificance of responsibility, then maintaining a stronger sense of responsibility (because that is what is needed) in some other area will be difficult. In short, if we think of Stephen's debate between science and law, his answer – that science is science and the law is the law – seems to sell the issue short. Third, the fear that accompanies pushing arguments back in this way is that it leaves them vulnerable to clashing first principles. Think of the debate between Rawls (1971) and Nozick (1974). Rawls presents us with one picture of our political lives: a picture in which we live together and, in some sense, share one another's fate. Nozick presents us with a picture in which we think of ourselves as separate co-operators, lucky or unlucky in our capacities. Rawls and Nozick do not begin with different conceptions of responsibility (one determinist, the other libertarian), and then derive from this different theories of social justice. Rather, they start at the other end, asking what is the proper way for citizens to interact with one another and with the State. Their answers to this question dictate that social practices will treat people as responsible in different ways.

Looking at these methodological (and substantive) concerns, one procedure comes immediately to mind as designed to cope with the kinds of difficulties involved. That is the procedure of wide reflective equilibrium, with its combination of broad ethical enquiry and space for other theoretical considerations. As Norman Daniels, who has developed reflective equilibrium from its Rawlsian beginnings, puts it, it is the 'marshaling of the broadest evidence and critical scrutiny' that is the attraction of wide reflective equilibrium:

> We not only must work back and forth between principles and judgments about particular cases . . . but we must bring to bear all theoretical considerations that have relevance to the acceptability of the principles as well as the particular judgments. These theoretical considerations may be empirical or they may be moral. One task of ethical theory, then, is to show how work in the social sciences, for example, has a bearing on moral considerations. Ethical theory helps us to expand the kinds of considerations that count as evidence for or against our moral views at all levels of generality. Wide reflective equilibrium, then, forces us to elaborate moral theory in many directions and to attend to the broadest range of considerations and arguments that could count as evidence for our moral beliefs; it forces us to examine the structure of this far-flung system of beliefs and theories. (Daniels 1996: 6)

Invoking the language of reflective equilibrium has one further advantage. It seems to me a danger of a Peter Strawsonian or Williamsite position that one thinks of responsibility as simply emerging from a proper understanding of the purposes of a given practice. Thus, once one has argued for a particular understanding of the criminal law, for example, the notion of responsibility relevant to the criminal law will follow straightforwardly. But that cannot be right. Many of our practices are suffused with ideas of responsibility. So, to reflect on the proper purpose of those practices is also to reflect on the idea of responsibility (as is clear from the three positions on strict liability described above). What is needed, then, is a dialogue – or, in the language of reflective equilibrium, a working back and forth – between the practices and the ideas of responsibility embedded within them. This is undoubtedly a challenge. The only test of whether it can be done without falling back into metaphysical debates (or at all) is to try it.

6   Conclusion

It might seem that this long chapter offers little more than just another twirl on Galen Strawson's carousel. We make judgements of responsibility, but, particularly when these judgements carry important consequences for individuals, we worry that responsibility is impossible because, however the person acted now, they cannot properly be held responsible for all the causes of their action stretching back to before they were born. Not so, says the compatibilist, because we can make sense of responsibility without needing this kind of radical freedom. Yet the worry is that even if the compatibilist is successful, the kind of responsibility that can be rescued is not the kind that is needed; it is not responsibility in the fully-fledged sense we need to be confident when the consequences for someone (perhaps ourselves) might be very grave. Thus, we are returned to the need to formulate some 'true' or 'ultimate' responsibility, but that is impossible.

I think this circular pattern of demands, responses, and worries captures something very important about how we use the concept of responsibility.[22] Compatibilists are right in thinking that responsibility can be compatible with the truth of determinism and/or the Causal Thesis, but that should not lead us to ignore the threat described by Galen Strawson. The legitimacy of our practices of holding people responsible may depend, for us, on a strong sense of responsibility that cannot be rescued by compatibilists. If so, then we need to work – just as the method of reflective equilibrium suggests – at both ends: looking at what we are doing in our practices, as well as what can be delivered by an account of responsibility. Moreover, we must be open to the thought that some of our practices may need to be rethought if compatibilist responsibility cannot fill the hole left by the impossibility of our being 'truly' or 'ultimately' responsible.

That said, we must not lose sight of what compatibilism has to contribute. Normal, competent human beings have the capacity to reflect on their immediate impulses and desires and on the values and principles that inform the way they live their lives. This characterization of agency is what normally underwrites the language of responsibility in liberal societies. Compatibilism rightly emphasizes this capacity and the way in which its successful operation depends on a particular relationship obtaining between elements of agents' mental economies. However, that these things are important to our practices of holding responsible does not mean, as we have seen, that they can be combined in an account of what it is 'really' to be responsible. Moreover, and most importantly, we should not be misled by their importance into thinking that the best way to answer the question, 'When is it fair to hold someone responsible?' is by first trying to give an independent account of 'When they are really responsible'. Instead, what is suggested here is that there is an intimate, reciprocal relationship between our ideas of fairness and of responsibility.

3
Responsibility within Distributive Justice

1 Distributive Justice

In the last chapter it was suggested that a productive way to think about the idea of responsibility is to consider the contexts in which judgements of responsibility are made. Moreover, what was recommended is that we move between accounts of responsibility and our practices of holding people responsible. The focus of this chapter is on our practices of, and judgements of responsibility within, distributive justice.

Theories of distributive justice concern the distribution of scarce resources and opportunities among the individuals in a given society (or, in the case of international distributive justice, amongst the people(s) of the world). When such theories are also described as theories of social justice, what is usually meant is that the objects of evaluation are the policies and institutional arrangements on the basis of which distributions are established (what Rawls called 'the basic structure of society').

These definitions are not fixed, and the relationship of this kind of theorizing to that concerned with the traditional virtue of justice is complex. Plato and Aristotle famously thought in terms of just city-states as well as just persons, but it is probably right to say that traditionally justice has most often been thought of as a virtue of individuals. A just person behaved a certain way in relation to his friends, strangers, fellow citizens, and so on. He possessed what is often considered to be the standard formal account of the concept of justice: 'the constant and perpetual will to give each his due'.[1] Of course, this view of justice can be extended fairly easily to social justice. A just situation obtains when social institutions give rise to the outcome that people have what is due to them and do not have what is not due to them.[2]

If justice is a matter of people having what is due to them and not having what is not, then it would seem that there is a straightforward account of social justice that follows: the institutions of society are just when they work so as to ensure that each person has what is due to him. The trouble is that how we establish what is due to each person is an area of significant conflict and controversy. Some people, for example, believe that what is due to themselves and others is determined by God, and that those who belong to God's chosen people are due different things from those due to others. Other people believe that what people are due ought to depend on their needs, on the one hand, and their productive capacities, on the other.

Even amongst those who would normally be called 'liberal' political theorists (and practitioners) there is considerable disagreement about what is due to people. It is possible to be a liberal and to think that people are due a certain basic set of inalienable rights (which may be more or less extensive), or that people are due what they need, or that people are due equal welfare, or equal resources. This list can be expanded, so what is it that characterizes a 'liberal' position given this diversity? In fact, characterizing liberalism is not at all easy, and the term is now so widely and loosely used that it is probably not very useful even to try to do so.[3] In what follows, an account is offered of a particular strand of liberalism, liberal egalitarianism. What marks out this strand (and perhaps liberalism more generally) is a commitment to the fundamental equality of persons.[4]

The idea of *fundamental* equality captures a sense in which persons are regarded as equal just in virtue of being persons.

Thus, what is upheld is the view that persons are equal in some important sense despite the manifest differences between them in their heights, talents, productive capacities, personalities, and so on. Moreover, what is rejected is any argument that appeals to the idea that persons are fundamentally *un*equal in virtue of such things as race, gender, relationship to God, and caste. There is, then, a relationship between this idea of liberalism and the kinds of commitments famously made in the US's Declaration of Independence and the French Declaration of the Rights of Man that 'all men are created equal' and 'are born and remain free and equal in rights'.

It follows from this that for liberal egalitarians there is an important connection between justice and equality. Justice, as we have seen, concerns giving people what is due to them. Equality concerns treating alike things that are relevantly alike (and treating differently things that are relevantly different). The default position for liberal egalitarians, then, is that persons are fundamentally equal, and this equality is relevant to justice. Thus, there is an initial case for saying that justice requires giving persons like treatment (treating them as equals) because all persons are relevantly alike. In so far as there are to be any justified movements away from equality, then, the burden of proof is on those who would justify inequalities to show that there are *relevant* differences between the persons receiving unequal treatment.[5]

As already noted, this united commitment to the equality of persons does not lead to a united front on what is due to people. Indeed, a popular way of thinking about the recent history of Anglo-American political philosophy is to think of it as a series of debates about how best to understand what is required by a commitment to treat persons as equals (for example, does it require an equal distribution of rights, or of welfare, or of status, or, perhaps, of all three?). However, the focus of this book is responsibility, and there is one strand of contemporary theorizing about justice – sometimes called 'responsibility-sensitive egalitarianism', sometimes 'luck egalitarianism' – that has recently enjoyed a dominant position in the literature and in which the concept of responsibility has played a central role. Its development, more than anything else, has led to increased attention being paid to the role of responsibility within distributive justice. Moreover, the development of responsibility-sensitive egalitarianism has been hailed by its proponents as *politically* as well as *philosophically* important. Before considering the position in detail, it is worth pausing to consider why this is so. To do this requires a brief look at the recent relationship of theorizing about politics and political practice in the USA and the UK.

2   Theory and Practice

John Rawls's death in November 2002 led to many respectful obituaries in the US and UK press, but it did not prompt a response from the British Prime Minister (as had the death of Isaiah Berlin five years before) or any comment from the US President. This is striking. Rawls was the greatest political philosopher of the twentieth century, and the most important one writing in English since Hobbes (in the seventeenth century). His subject was often politics, in particular the contemporary politics of the USA, yet his writings and ideas had little identifiable impact on politics. More than that, as we saw in chapter 1, for the entire period after the 1971 publication of his masterpiece, *A Theory of Justice*, politics in the USA and the UK moved further and further away from the positions outlined in that book. In 1979, Margaret Thatcher came to power in the UK, followed in 1980 by Ronald Reagan's electoral success in the USA. Since then, despite the victory of ostensibly left of centre parties in both countries, the whole political spectrum has moved to the right.

One obvious explanation for Rawls's absence from politics arises from this gap between his thinking and the political ideologies of those in power. Put bluntly, Rawls's views were to the left, and the dominant positions in recent political debates have ranged from centre right to right. Yet, it is hard to believe that this is the whole explanation. Politicians are not always scrupulous when invoking intellectual figures as their allies. Thus, thinkers such as Milton Friedman, Robert Nozick, and Friedrich Hayek were routinely invoked by the right (particularly in the 1980s), despite the fact that Friedman explicitly denied that Reagan and Thatcher had implemented monetarist policies, and Nozick and Hayek must have detested the moralizing tones and many of the policies of both administrations. In short, politicians on the right were happy to invoke the names and slogans of several of the century's great thinkers of the right, without paying too much attention to the details, whereas left-leaning politicians eschewed Rawls. Yet, 'Justice as fairness' is a pretty good slogan and a better bumper sticker than injunctions about governing supply-side economics (a mantra from Milton Friedman) that were the staple of Thatcher and Reagan.

The puzzle, then, is this: why were Rawls (and Rawlsians) ignored even by those – like Blair, Clinton, and Schroeder – who claimed to be on the left and who saw themselves as revitalizing the left (through what was initially termed 'the third way')? That Rawls was to the left of them is no doubt part of the explanation, but for the reasons just discussed, it is not entirely convincing.

One answer to this puzzle was offered in a paper on liberalism in philosophy and politics by the philosopher Samuel Scheffler. Scheffler noted that part of the attack sustained by the left in, and after, the Thatcher and Reagan elections was based on the perception that the policies of the left threatened to undermine traditional notions of individual agency and responsibility (2001: 13). The accusations (briefly surveyed in chapter 1) have become familiar: in the sphere of criminal justice, liberals emphasize the social causes of crime, and not the individual criminal and the individual victim. A connected claim, in relation to both criminal justice and broader social issues, is that liberals reinterpret what were traditionally seen as vices as diseases or addictions. Thus, chronic gamblers and drinkers are victims of inherited addictive personality disorders; the serial adulterer is treated for 'sex addiction'; and the wife who intentionally kills (rather than leaves) her abusive husband is acquitted on grounds of 'battered woman syndrome'. In the provision of social welfare, liberal policies stand accused of, first, failing to discriminate between genuine cases of hardship caused by misfortune and feckless laziness, and second, of creating a culture of dependency because of the skewed incentives created by social welfare provision (see Scheffler 2001: 14–15; sect. 1.2 above).

Whatever the truth of these allegations (and Scheffler makes it clear that he does not endorse them), they provided one of the cornerstones of the powerful assault on left of centre, social democratic parties in the UK and the USA. Moreover, this was not just an assault from without. The timing of Scheffler's piece is in this regard interesting. It was, he says, 'written in 1991, toward the end of a twelve-year period during which the Republican party controlled the American Presidency' (2001: 3). It was published in the autumn of 1992. In November of that year this domination of US politics by the Republicans came to an end when Bill Clinton recaptured the White House for the Democrats. However, the foundation of Clinton's policy agenda was 'to emphasise traditional notions of individual responsibility' (Scheffler 2001: 3) and to consign those policies perceived to undermine responsibility to the back burner. A similar political strategy brought Tony Blair electoral success in the UK in 1997.

The problem, Scheffler argued, lay in the inability of liberal political philosophy to come to terms with desert and individual responsibility. That is, just when the political left needed a vision of society to offer as an alternative to, and a defence against, that tendered by the right, the philosophical left was developing a vision which seemed to play into the hands of the right by affirming the irrelevance of desert and individual responsibility. This thesis is examined below, but nothing said there disproves the conjecture that those left-wing politicians who read Rawls – or, more likely, had his views summarized for them by political advisors – may well have thought 'with friends like that who needs enemies'.

Moreover, the perceived development of liberal political theory, in which it is seen as having incorporated desert, has been hailed as of great political importance. Again, whether it is so is something discussed below.

If Scheffler is right, at least in his political speculations, individual responsibility is an important political value and one that was perceived to be missing from liberal political theory until the development of responsibility-sensitive egalitarianism. In what follows, the idea of responsibility-sensitive egalitarianism is examined, and then the story of its origins in Rawls's *A Theory of Justice* is considered. As we shall see, the philosophical problems discussed in chapter 2 emerge in this strand of liberal political theory.

3   Responsibility-sensitive Egalitarianism

If liberals adopt a default position of equality, then, as noted above, differences in the treatment of people will stand in need of justification. Any such justification must appeal to *relevant* differences between the recipients. As noted in chapter 2, the most influential school of thought in contemporary liberal political philosophy, responsibility-sensitive egalitarianism, holds that differences between people's holdings can be justified if they arise from different *choices* and cannot be justified if they arise from luck or *chance*. 'The concern of distributive justice', as Richard Arneson puts it, 'is to compensate individuals for misfortune.' He goes on:

> [S]ome people are blessed with good luck, some are cursed with bad luck, and it is the responsibility of society – of all of us regarded collectively – to alter the distribution of goods and evils that arises from the jumble of lotteries that constitutes human life as we know it. Some are lucky to be born wealthy, or into a favorable socializing environment, or with a tendency to be charming and intelligent and persevering and the like. These people are likely to be successful in the economic marketplace and to achieve success in other important ways over the course

of their lives. On the other hand, some people are, as we say, born to lose. Distributive justice stipulates that the lucky should transfer some or all of their gains due to luck to the unlucky.[6]

This idea, as Elizabeth Anderson points out, combines two moral premisses: 'that people should be compensated for undeserved misfortunes and that the compensation should come only from that part of others' good fortune that is undeserved' (Anderson 1999: 290). The second of these reflects the significance of choice and responsibility: in justice, people are entitled to that part of their holdings that is not the result of good fortune, but is rather the product of their choices and actions for which they can claim responsibility (hence Barry's two principles of distribution discussed in section 2.1 above).

As has been discussed already, this idea is philosophically and politically appealing. Philosophically, it belongs to an important Kantian tradition in liberalism, which focuses on autonomy and agency. Politically, it offers the left a way of responding to the kinds of accusations made by the right and discussed above: accusations that the left is insufficiently robust about individual choice, ambition, and responsibility. A responsibility-sensitive egalitarianism seems to be just what is needed to counter these allegations. Indeed, when Ronald Dworkin first formulated his account of responsibility-sensitive egalitarianism, it was warmly greeted by the (sometime Marxist) philosopher G. A. Cohen in overtly political terms, as incorporating within it 'the most powerful idea in the arsenal of the anti-egalitarian right: the idea of choice and responsibility' (Cohen 1989: 933). Moreover, Dworkin himself, when picking a passage of the book for the back cover of *Sovereign Virtue* (and so, one must assume, offering an overall assessment of the point of the book), chose to emphasize its political value. The quotation reads:

> Politicians are now anxious to endorse what they call a 'new' liberalism, or a 'third' way. . . . The old egalitarians insisted that a political community has a collective responsibility to show equal concern for all its citizens, but they defined that equal concern in a way that ignored those citizens' personal responsibilities.

Conservatives – new and old – insisted on that personal responsibility, but they have defined it so as to ignore the collective responsibility. The choice between these two mistakes is an unnecessary as well as an unattractive one. If the argument that follows is sound, we can achieve a unified account of equality and responsibility that respects both. If that is the third way, then it should be our way. (2000: 7 and back cover)

In addition to these advantages, responsibility-sensitive egalitarianism seems generally in tune with much of our ordinary moral thinking. Discrimination on the basis of such unchosen features of the person as race and gender is widely condemned. Similarly, it is commonly thought that equally talented people with equal motivation ought to have equal access to positions of advantage. On the other side, so to speak, it is thought that those who choose to work hard and put in extra effort are entitled to greater rewards than those who choose not to do so.

Thus, it should be clear how responsibility-sensitive egalitarianism can be thought of as a response to the political problem highlighted by Scheffler. That said, the degree of overlap between ordinary moral thinking and responsibility-sensitive egalitarianism (and so its political usefulness) will vary depending on what is counted by the egalitarian as choice and what as chance. Thus, those responsibility-sensitive egalitarians who think that people's natural talents and dispositions (for example, the disposition to work hard) are matters of *chance* go well beyond ordinary morality and beyond what might be politically useful.

The appeal of responsibility-sensitive egalitarianism, then, is very great. It draws on an important tradition in liberal philosophy in which persons are thought of as choosing agents; it allows egalitarians to respond to right-wing critics; it connects with much in ordinary moral thinking; and it is intuitively plausible that justice has something to do with people getting what they are responsible for and not benefiting or being burdened by good and bad luck. However, as we have seen, responsibility is a complex and problematic idea.

3.1   Choice and chance (or Dworkin versus Cohen)

Dworkin writes that in his book *Sovereign Virtue* he uses the 'key distinction between chance and choice' in answering the question of 'when and how far is it right that individuals bear the disadvantages or misfortunes of their own situations themselves, and when is it right . . . that others . . . relieve them from or mitigate the consequences of these disadvantages?' The reason he does so, he says, is because 'our judgments about personal and collective responsibility are dominated by [that] distinction' (Dworkin 2000: 287).

Of course, as Dworkin admits, choice and chance can be distinguished in different ways. He thus needs to give some particular content to the choice/chance distinction, and he does so in distinguishing between persons' mental and physical capacities and their personalities. He writes, 'the political community should aim to erase or mitigate differences between people in their personal resources – [in their] health, strength, and talent – but should not aim to mitigate or compensate for differences in personality – for differences traceable to the fact that some people's tastes and ambitions are expensive and other people's cheap, for instance' (2000: 286).

What is curious about this is that when discussing his overall project Dworkin is, as we have seen, insistent on the choice/chance distinction. It is, as he writes in the passage quoted above, 'key', and it 'dominates' our judgements of responsibility. Yet, the distinction between personality and personal resources does not mention choice or chance (and is, at best, orthogonal to the choice/chance distinction). This was a point made forcefully in a reply to Dworkin by Cohen.

Cohen, as mentioned above, welcomed Dworkin's approach as politically useful, in that it could incorporate desert and responsibility within liberal egalitarianism. However, Cohen (and others) allege that Dworkin's cut between personality and personal resources fails to capture the significance of choice and the arbitrariness of (brute) luck that motivates Dworkin's (and the responsibility-sensitive egalitarian) project. Cohen insists that 'the right cut is between responsibility and bad luck' (1989: 922) even where this cuts across personality and personal resources.

An example might be useful here, and, fortunately, one is at the heart of the debate between Dworkin and Cohen. The example – this being a debate between philosophers – concerns Louis, who has expensive tastes (for plovers' eggs and pre-phylloxera claret). Louis, let us say, gets the same welfare from these expensive goods as someone else gets from regular hens' eggs and cheap wine. Thus, if 'welfare' were the relevant measure of equality, then a liberal egalitarian society would have to transfer resources to Louis so that he can satisfy his expensive tastes. After much sophisticated discussion, Dworkin argues that any such redistribution cannot be defended as part of an adequate account of treating people as equals. Thus, Dworkin concludes, equality of welfare is an inadequate theory of distributional equality (2000: 48ff). There is, in Brian Barry's words, 'something mildly crazy about the idea that an ideally just situation would be one where people who needed champagne and caviar to get to the average level of consumer satisfaction would get more money' (1991: 154).[7]

This conclusion is consistent with Dworkin's cut between personal resources and personality. However, it may not be consistent with the more basic cut between responsibility and bad luck. For Cohen, who wants to maintain that straightforward cut, we must distinguish, say, Louis I who *chooses* to develop his tastes for plovers' eggs and fine claret and Louis II who, through no choice of his own, comes to have such tastes (call this the 'unchosen tastes' argument). 'I distinguish', writes Cohen, 'among expensive tastes according to whether or not the bearer can reasonably be held responsible for them', where responsibility is to be determined by voluntariness (Cohen 1989: 923). Similarly, John Roemer argues that it would be wrong for people to be held 'accountable for their choices, even if they follow from preferences which were in part or entirely formed under influences beyond their control' (1998: 19).

In addition to the unchosen tastes argument, Louis (I or II) does not control the tastes and choices of others, nor does he control the weather, soil types, or the growing characteristics of grapes. He is not responsible either for the relative scarcity of plovers compared to hens. In short, even if it were the case that Louis was responsible for his tastes, he would not be responsible for their being expensive (call this the 'expensiveness' argument; see Cohen 1989: 927).

The lines of dispute are clear. If what matters is to distinguish things that are down to choice from those that are a matter of chance, then, Cohen alleges, Dworkin's cut is too restrictive. If, *ex hypothesi*, Louis II simply found himself with his expensive tastes and Louis I deliberately cultivated his, then it seems to violate the initial motivation to eliminate luck from justice to hold that they are relevantly alike. More generally, the claim that the society should not, as Dworkin puts it, aim 'to mitigate or compensate for differences in personality' (2000: 286) fails to appreciate the degree to which our personalities are beyond our control. As Rawls puts it (albeit in a different context), 'even the willingness to make an effort, to try, and so to be deserving in the ordinary sense is itself dependent upon happy family and social circumstances' (Rawls 1971: 74). Dworkin's own slogan for liberal theory, that it seeks to be 'endowment-insensitive' and 'ambition-sensitive' (2000: 108), can thus be turned against him (or so his critics allege). For what it reveals is Dworkin's failure to appreciate the degree to which ambition, and other personality traits, are a matter of endowment, and thus a matter of luck.

4   The Problematic Nature of Responsibility-sensitive Egalitarianism

Given the compelling force of Cohen's argument that his cut is more faithful to Dworkin's (and responsibility-sensitive egalitarianism's) grounding idea of distinguishing choice and chance than is Dworkin's own distinction between preferences and resources, it might be asked why Dworkin, and most other liberal egalitarians, resist Cohen's straightforward cut between responsibility and bad luck. After all, as we have seen, the distinction between choice and chance goes to the heart of the *liberal* nature of liberal egalitarianism and the elimination of the latter to the Kantian aspiration to purge any element of luck from the determination of what we deserve. In short, we have seen that the choice/chance distinction is central to the responsibility-sensitive egalitarian project. Dworkin himself endorses it as underpinning the arguments of his book. Yet, offered a straightforward cut based on choice and chance, Dworkin (and many other responsibility-sensitive egalitarians) resists, preferring, instead, to distinguish personality and personal resources; a cut that does not even attempt to reflect the choice/chance distinction. Why?

The answer lies in the worry that, taken in Cohen's straightforward sense, the cut between choice and chance is both too deep and too wide. Moreover, it threatens to immerse distributive justice in all of the problems of responsibility discussed in chapter 2.

4.1   Width problems within responsibility-sensitive egalitarianism

The choice/chance distinction threatens to be too wide both in the sense that it encompasses too much and in the sense that it is too sweeping. Luck is pervasive, and people's lives are often blighted (or successful) in areas where questions of compensation and distributive justice are not typically thought to be appropriate. An agent might have the misfortune to be grumpy, without friends, or might go through life feeling lonely having had the bad luck not to meet the right man or woman (or a man or woman from that set) with whom to share that life. Nevertheless, liberal egalitarians typically do not think such things candidates for compensation, and not because it would be *impractical* (although it would), but because it would be *inappropriate*. Consider Elizabeth Anderson's dystopian vision of a society governed by the distinction between choice and chance. She envisages a 'State Equality Board' that writes to 'the ugly and socially awkward':

> How sad that you are so repulsive to people around you that no-one wants to be your friend or lifetime companion. We won't make it up to you by being your friend or your marriage partner – we have our own freedom of association to exercise – but you can console yourself in your miserable loneliness by consuming these material goods that we, the beautiful and charming ones, will provide. And who knows? Maybe you won't be such a loser in love once potential dates see how rich you are. (Anderson 1999: 305)

Anderson's example also catches the sense in which the choice/chance distinction is too sweeping. Just as we would not think of the repulsive as owed compensation, so we would not necessarily hold that someone who had recklessly made himself repulsive should be left to pick up whatever consequences follow. In positing that choice leads to full responsibility, responsibility-sensitive egalitarianism has within it what Scheffler calls a 'moralistic' strain, by which he means 'a deformation or disfiguration of the moral' (2005: 14). As Scheffler writes:

> [M]ost people do not insist . . . that someone who makes a bad decision thereby forfeits all claims to assistance. They do not take such a sweeping view either in matters of personal morality or in political contexts [footnote omitted]. In their personal lives, for example, they do not refuse to comfort a friend whose foolish, but voluntarily undertaken, romance has come to a painful end . . . . [I]n wider social and political contexts, [m]ost people do not believe that an indigent defendant should be denied legal representation, even if her inability to afford an attorney was the result of bad financial planning or imprudent credit-card use . . . nor do they believe that people whose poverty has resulted from poor financial decision-making should be denied emergency medical care or assistance in obtaining food or shelter. (Scheffler 2005: 15)

For Scheffler, policies that did maintain this kind of blanket responsibility for the costs of bad choices would be 'harsh, unforgiving, insensitive to context' and, most importantly, 'moralistic' (2005: 15).

It may be that width problems can be ameliorated within responsibility-sensitive egalitarianism. One might, for example, try to circumscribe the scope of justice by appeal to other values such as privacy, or by appeal to a kind of social division of labour that allocates certain problems to the State and others to friends and family.[8] It may even be that they are not really problems at all. After all, what is being appealed to here is the thought that 'we egalitarians' would not endorse compensation for the ugly or leave entirely to his own devices someone responsible for his own repulsiveness. But perhaps we would (or should), and a properly responsibility-sensitive egalitarian society would have this kind of width. Depth problems, however, are more fundamental.

4.2   Depth problems within responsibility-sensitive egalitarianism

The cut between choice and chance threatens to be too deep because, as we have seen from the discussion of Galen Strawson in chapter 2, people's (apparent) choices are often (perhaps always) dictated by features of themselves (their tastes, ambitions, personalities, etc.) and the world (their options, other people's choices, etc.) that they did not choose. That is, the threat of regression haunts the choice/chance distinction. For surely if choice is so critical, then it will matter whether apparent choices are themselves based on other choices or on chance? Thus, for example, when Roemer writes that for people to be accountable for their choices, those choices must follow from preferences which were not 'in part or entirely formed under influences beyond their control' (quoted above), he seems to make accountability impossible. *All* our preferences are formed (certainly in part, if not entirely) under genetic and social influences beyond our control.

In 'foregrounding' (Cohen 1989: 922) choice and chance, then, Cohen's cut threatens, as he puts it, to 'land political philosophy in the morass of the free-will problem'. For whilst Dworkin's 'distinction between preferences and resources is not metaphysically deep', it is, 'by contrast, awesomely difficult to identify what represents *genuine* choice' (Cohen 1989: 934, emphasis original). It seems, then, that the political and philosophical benefits of responsibility-sensitive egalitarianism either come at a price or do not materialize at all. Encompassing responsibility threatens to extend the State's role beyond what is legitimate and to involve the State in moralistic judgements of its citizens. Moreover, rather than incorporate the value of agency, responsibility-sensitive egalitarianism threatens to undermine the whole possibility of agency by depending on an unrealizable metaphysics of responsibility.[9]

However, if we think back to chapter 2, a solution might suggest itself. Taking the significance of choice so seriously, whilst attractive for the reasons described in this chapter, seems to endow choice with an unsupportable 'enormous political and economic weight' (Scheffler 2005: 12). Choice makes all the difference, and this could only be straightforwardly true if responsibility-sensitive egalitarianism endorses a Galen Strawson-like view of the metaphysical significance of choice (whilst, of course, maintaining a very un-Galen Strawson view on its possibility). However, and again as discussed in chapter 2, it seems at least possible that choice need not have this status for the idea of responsibility to get some purchase, and that the kind of freedom needed for responsibility need not be one that does not involve any role for chance.

5   Semi-choicism

The problems identified above stem, as we have seen, from a commitment to choice and chance as critical in deciding on relevant differences between fundamentally equal agents. However, as noted above, whilst Dworkin endorses the language of choice and chance, he does not actually deploy the distinction. Indeed, he goes further and explicitly denies that choice need be 'deep'. 'The conventional distinction we all make between circumstances and personality', he writes, 'does not assume that we have chosen our personality, *and so would not be undermined by any argument, no matter how general or metaphysical, that we could not have chosen it*' (Dworkin 2000: 294, emphasis added).

What is so striking about this – in particular about the final sentence – is that it seems to pull the ground out from underneath the original dispute. As we have seen, in that dispute Cohen took issue with Dworkin's personality/personal resources cut precisely because that cut could not accommodate the difference between chosen and unchosen expensive tastes. The main thrust of Cohen's argument was that, given the fundamental moral significance of choice and chance, Louis is only consequentially responsible for his tastes if he chose to develop them. The cut between personality and resources is thus too blunt precisely because we ought to be concerned with the degree to which the agent is responsible – that is to say (in the terms of the choice/chance distinction), chooses – the relevant aspects of his personality (and the degree to which, say, these 'sneak up on him'). Much of Cohen's argument is dedicated to showing that Dworkin's own commitment to the moral significance of the choice/chance distinction is such that Dworkin should recognize the morally relevant difference between chosen and unchosen tastes. Yet, in reply, Dworkin argues that an agent's consequential responsibility for her personality is unaffected by choice, and would be unaffected even if the agent *could not* have exercised choice in forming her personality. Clearly, then, no matter what Dworkin says about the choice/chance distinction being the 'key' one that 'dominates' our judgements of responsibility, he does not believe that in any straightforward sense. What, then, is going on, both in Dworkin and in responsibility-sensitive egalitarianism?

One possible answer has been christened (and affirmed) by Brian Barry as 'semi-choicism'. The idea is to retain the importance of choice, but without investing in choice the kind of metaphysical significance that, as we have seen in chapter 2 and in the depth criticisms of responsibility-sensitive egalitarianism, makes it problematic. This can be done by combining the Cohenite thought that 'people are responsible for the outcomes of actions only if they are responsible for the preferences from which those actions flow' with the anti-Cohenite (anti-choice) position that *denies* that 'responsibility for preferences [is] dependent on their being subject to choice' (Barry 1991: 156). This, of course, delivers political philosophy from the morass of the free-will problem and the threat of regression, and it delivers what are, in the views of many people, the right results.

The question, though, is why we should hold choice to be so important at one level and irrelevant at another. That is, although as noted in chapter 2, we might agree that choice need not go all the way down, if so much about people's lives and entitlements is going to depend on their choices at some point, it seems legitimate to worry about the point just back from the one picked out as making all the difference and that leads us towards the regression problem. To avoid this, something other than choice must make the critical difference. Barry's suggestion, endorsed separately by Dworkin, is that agents can be held responsible for actions that result from their choices where their choices result from preferences *not* that they chose, but with which they identify (whether or not they chose them being irrelevant) (Barry 1991: 156; Dworkin 2000: 187ff).

The argument that an agent's identifying with his preferences makes the critical difference has some attractions in addition to the undoubted virtue of getting political philosophy out of the morass of the free-will problem. It seems consonant with our ideas of the respect owed to agents to pay attention to those aspects of their personalities that they take to be part of their identity. Thus, there would be something disrespectful in treating a religious believer, whose beliefs were particularly guilt inducing and welfare destroying, as roughly equivalent to someone with a disability and so entitled to compensation. More informally, if we think of justice as compensating for bad luck, there is something odd in compensating someone for something that they do not regret and would not relinquish.

However, despite these advantages, the identification argument cannot do the work (at least, it cannot do all of it). If we ask what is the relevant difference between two agents justly due different treatment, the answer cannot be one that centres on identification any more than it can be one that centres on a straightforward account of the choice/chance distinction. Identifying with one's tastes, choices, and preferences and consequential responsibility seem to come apart too often and in different ways.

On the one hand, as already noted, if choice is so important, as both Barry and Dworkin think it is, then the absence of choice ought to be troubling wherever it occurs. The content Anglican whose parents, though believers themselves, allowed their child a liberal education, the 'indoctrinated' member of a religious cult, and JoJo (from the example given in chapter 2) all may identify with their preferences, and their preferences may be said to be (to some degree) unchosen. Yet, they are arguably not all responsible to the same degree (or, if they are, something other than the fact that they identify with their preferences is going to have to do the work). On the other hand, it is not clear that consequential responsibility disappears with the agent's renouncing some aspect of his personality. A selfish person who behaves shoddily towards another is not necessarily relieved of responsibility for this by saying how much he wishes he were not selfish, even if he is sincere.

Finally, it is worth noting that different people identify in different ways with similar features. This is problematic for someone like Dworkin, because it is clear that some people will identify with their unchosen talents and abilities, which Dworkin would, of course, count as merely amongst their circumstances (cf. Scheffler 2005: 11). It is also more generally problematic because people may disagree profoundly about the nature of some human feature. Thus, there is a controversial debate amongst those who are deaf about whether deafness should be thought of as a disability or an identity. As Anthony Appiah put it, making a similar complaint about the identification argument in a review of *Sovereign Virtue*: 'For many deaf people . . . their deafness is not a limitation but a parameter: a condition becomes an identity – the deaf become the Deaf. . . . Similarly, for Pavarotti, talent as a tenor is not a circumstance of his life but one of its parameters, just as Michael Jordan's athleticism and Ronald Dworkin's philosophical skills are for them' (Appiah 2001: §5).

6   Liberalism and Responsibility-sensitive Egalitarianism

There are two themes that have recurred in this and the first two chapters. First is the seeming importance of the choice/ chance distinction. Deploying it within justice appears, as I have said, in tune with our intuitions and with our philosophical and political commitments. However, and second, that distinction is treacherous. It cannot be given a straightforward interpretation for reasons prefigured in chapter 2. If choice is so important – if it is to carry the weight of making all the difference to what is justly due to people – then it is a worry that we cannot have chosen those aspects of ourselves that now result in our current choices, and so our current choices do not seem to be 'ours' in the right way. The semi-choicist alternative is attractive because it puts a halt on the regress, but as it remains within the language of choice and chance, the significance it gives to choice at one level sits uncomfortably with its disregard for the absence of choice at another. Moreover, some argument would be needed about just what replaces choice at the level of preferences (or, in Dworkinian language, 'personality'), and the argument from identification is problematic. Perhaps the answer lies, then, in revisiting that fundamental distinction (and in so doing finding a different way of accommodating the attractions of the identification argument).

Given the discussion in chapter 2, there is reason to be sceptical about the prospects for political philosophy (and practice) if it merely replaces an unsophisticated chance/ choice distinction with a more sophisticated theory of responsibility such as a 'mesh' theory or a 'reasons-responsiveness' account of the type offered by Wallace and Fischer and Ravizza. One purpose of such accounts, of course, is to avoid the kind of reliance on choice that gives rise to worries about regression. But it is worth recalling the arguments of chapter 2 in the light of the discussion of the debate between Dworkin and Cohen.

In chapter 2, a contrast was drawn between ahistorical mesh theories and both ahistorical and historical reasons-responsiveness theories. In many ways, the debate between Dworkin and Cohen mirrors that between ahistorical mesh theorists and their critics (cf. Arneson 2003: 251–6). For Dworkin, whether someone is properly held responsible is decided by asking whether his actions flow in the right way from aspects of his personality with which he identifies. However, just as critics of mesh theories hold that the mesh can be created by responsibility-undermining factors, so Cohen alleges that Dworkin ignores the history of *how*, for example, Louis came to have (and to identify with) his expensive tastes.

Dworkin, in turn, alleges that Cohen's criticisms would lead to the loss of responsibility entirely, because it sets the standard of responsibility so high that no person could meet it given the truth of the Causal Thesis (or something like it). Cohen's argument, Dworkin complains, has 'indiscriminate force' (2000: 298; for a response, see Cohen 2004: 19). This worry – that we need to take history seriously, but that to do so threatens to land us with the regression problem, and so with the impossibility of moral responsibility – applies, too, to Fischer and Ravizza's reasons-responsiveness account (see ch. 2, sect. 4.2).

Of course, what is said in chapter 2 is not the final word on the matter of moral responsibility, and both mesh and reasons-responsiveness theorists will disagree with the rather bleak picture of the prospects for theories of moral responsibility painted there and here. At the same time, no one could deny that political philosophy, and political practice, is making great use of the idea of responsibility and of the choice/chance distinction, whilst their status in philosophical theory remains highly problematic. Indeed, the dialogue between Dworkin and Cohen can be represented, as it is above, as a spin on the Galen Strawsonian carousel discussed in chapter 2.

Moreover, the promise of this book is to look at the *use* made of the idea of responsibility within justice. Thus, it is surely worth pursuing the alternative approach, identified in chapter 2 with Bernard Williams, of asking first about distributive justice and what role responsibility has within our understandings and practices of distributive justice. To do so, we have to shake off – or at least treat much more warily – the conviction that justice *must* have at its heart the choice/chance distinction. One way to do this is to examine the claim that it is this distinction that underpins Rawls's *A Theory of Justice*.

6.1   Kymlicka on Rawls and responsibility-sensitive egalitarianism

According to Will Kymlicka, in his excellent survey of contemporary political philosophy (2002), the origins of contemporary responsibility-sensitive egalitarianism lie in Rawls's *A Theory of Justice* (1971). I will argue below for a different interpretation, but it is worth pausing to consider why Kymlicka thinks that responsibility-sensitive egalitarianism can be traced back to Rawls's arguments.

Rawls says very little about the concept of responsibility in *A Theory of Justice*.[10] Rather, it is his discussions of desert and equality of opportunity that provide the starting point for Kymlicka's tale. Rawls begins what Kymlicka calls his 'primary argument' (2002: 69) – that is, the argument of chapter 2 of *A Theory of Justice* – with the ideal of equal opportunity.[11] If inequalities are to be justified, they must arise from a situation in which opportunities are equal. Rawls's strategy, then, is to move through various interpretations of equal opportunity.

In the first, the 'system of natural liberty', there is only formal equality of opportunity in the sense that 'all have at least the same legal rights of access to all advantaged social positions'. This, Rawls argues, is unsatisfactory, because over time the distributions of inequalities will be 'strongly influenced' by 'natural talents and abilities . . . social circumstances and . . . accident and good fortune'. These things – things such as one's parents' social and economic position – are what Rawls calls 'arbitrary from a moral point of view' (all quotations from Rawls 1971: 72).

Given this arbitrariness, Rawls then considers what he calls 'the liberal interpretation' of equal opportunity, which adds to the lack of formal barriers to achieve advantage 'the principle of fair equality of opportunity'. He captures what is meant by this as follows:

> Assuming that there is a distribution of natural assets, those who are at the same level of talent and ability, and have the same willingness to use them, should have the same prospects of success regardless of the initial place in the social system, that is, irrespective of the income class into which they are born. In all sectors of society there should be roughly equal prospects of culture and achievement for everyone similarly motivated and endowed. The expectations of those with the same abilities and aspirations should not be affected by their social class. (Rawls 1971: 73)

As the name – 'the liberal interpretation' – suggests, this second stage appeals to familiar arguments. To see this, consider a society (Apartheid South Africa provides a close real-life approximation) in which there is legal discrimination against the black population. Blacks are legally restricted in where they can live, in the capital they can own, in the jobs for which they can apply, and so on. As a result, they are impoverished and lack basic goods such as reasonable nutrition and basic health care. Now imagine that in response to international pressure the Government of this country eradicates all formal, legal barriers to advantage. Of course, it remains true that the black population is impoverished, malnourished, and educated in poorly funded schools (if at all) relative to the white population. In these conditions, it would be grotesque to claim that the reformed society embodied equality of opportunity just because there were no longer any formal legal barriers to advancement. What the liberal interpretation adds to the system of natural liberty is simply the thought that underpins our reactions to this example. If there is to be fair equality of opportunity, then a morally arbitrary factor such as whether one is born black or white must by itself make no actual difference to one's prospects such that equally talented and willing blacks and whites must have roughly the same prospects of success.

Although familiar – and often part of the political rhetoric of politicians of both the right and the left – this argument is actually a radical one with considerable redistributive consequences. However, Rawls goes still further. He argues that whilst the liberal interpretation is an improvement on the system of natural liberty, it is still 'defective'. For, 'even if it works to perfection in eliminating the influence of social contingencies, it still permits the distribution of wealth and income to be determined by the natural distribution of abilities and talents'. This is problematic, according to Rawls, because if it is unfair for individuals to be disadvantaged by adverse social circumstances, then it is also unfair for them to be disadvantaged by adverse natural talents and abilities. As Rawls puts it, in the liberal interpretation 'distributive shares are decided by the outcome of the natural lottery', and the natural lottery, like its social equivalent, is 'arbitrary from a moral perspective'. In short, 'there is', according to Rawls, 'no more reason to permit the distribution of income and wealth to be settled by the distribution of natural assets than by historical and social fortune' (all quotations from Rawls 1971: 73–4).

For Rawls, then, the understandings of equal opportunity provided by both the system of natural liberty and the liberal interpretation are 'unstable', because 'from a moral standpoint . . . social contingencies [and] natural chance [are] equally arbitrary' (Rawls 1971: 74–5). We are thus led to what Rawls calls the 'democratic equality' conception of equal opportunity, 'which does not weight men's share in the benefits and burdens of social cooperation according to their social fortune or their luck in the natural lottery' (1971: 75). What this amounts to is, as Brian Barry puts it, 'equal opportunities for human beings stripped of all identifying characteristics, either genetic or environmental', and since all human characteristics are either genetic or environmental, this amounts to 'equal opportunity for entities that are not in any way distinguishable from one another', which is 'nothing other than equal prospects of success for all' or, in other terms, 'equality of outcomes' (Barry 1989: 223–4).

Whilst this completes Rawls's account of equal opportunity, his theory does not stop there. Famously, he goes on to argue that natural inequalities *can* legitimately lead to differences in outcomes, but only if these are to the greatest benefit of the least advantaged (the 'difference principle'):

> No one deserves his greater natural capacity nor merits a more favorable starting place in society. But it does not follow that one should eliminate these distinctions. There is another way to deal with them. The basic structure can be arranged so that these contingencies work for the good of the least fortunate. Thus we are led to the difference principle [social and economic inequalities are to be arranged so that they are to the greatest benefit of the least advantaged] if we wish to set up the social system so that no one gains or loses from his arbitrary place in the distribution of natural assets or his initial position in society without giving or receiving compensating advantages in return. (Rawls 1971: 102; the final formulation of the two principles, including the difference principle, is on p. 302)[12]

Although the above provides little more than a sketch of Rawls's equality-of-opportunity-based argument, it is sufficient for the purpose of understanding Kymlicka's particular reading of Rawls and his subsequent telling of the history of responsibility-sensitive egalitarianism. Right from the beginning, Kymlicka identifies Rawls's argument with the distinction between choice and chance. Thus, introducing the idea of equal opportunity, Kymlicka locates its appeal for Rawls in its ensuring 'that people's fate is determined by their choices, rather than their circumstances' (Kymlicka 2002: 58). He then identifies the underlying argument in Rawls's two moves – from natural liberty to the liberal interpretation and then to democratic equality – as an expansion of what counts as chance. The liberal interpretation, according to Kymlicka's reading of Rawls, correctly places social factors in the category of 'circumstances', but incorrectly ascribes natural talents and abilities to 'choice'. Once these are correctly reallocated to 'circumstances', we arrive at democratic equality.

Kymlicka thus argues that Rawls appeals to the 'choices–circumstances distinction' and imputes to Rawls a motivating goal of developing a theory that is what he calls (following Ronald Dworkin) 'ambition-sensitive' and 'endowment-insensitive' (Kymlicka 2002: 74; see Dworkin 1981: 311): that is, a theory which respects people's choices (ambitions), but does not allow people to be benefited or burdened by their natural or social endowments. This is to read Rawls as a responsibility-sensitive egalitarian, a reading that is further supported by appeal to Rawls's argument that people are responsible for their choices, which appears as part of his defence of social primary goods (rights, liberties, income and wealth, and so on) as the correct 'currency' of justice (Rawls 1971: sect. 15; cf. Kymlicka 2002: 74).

Having thus placed Rawls firmly within – and at the start of – the responsibility-sensitive egalitarian school, Kymlicka goes on to criticize Rawls as neither properly ambition-sensitive nor properly endowment-insensitive. Kymlicka argues that the difference principle, which requires that inequalities are allowed only when they are to the greatest benefit of the least advantaged, does not distinguish between those who are worst off because of their choices and those who are in that position because of chance. In failing to distinguish between these, then, the difference principle fails to be properly ambition-sensitive (Kymlicka 2002: 72–4). In addition, the difference principle concerns only primary *social* goods. It does not take into account differences in primary *natural* goods (such as health). Thus, within the terms of the difference principle, two people are equally well-off if they have identical bundles of primary social goods even if one is healthy and the other has a medical condition such that he requires expensive support and treatment. Thus, Kymlicka argues, the difference principle is not properly endowment-insensitive (2002: 70–2). What is needed, then, is a better ambition-sensitive, endowment-insensitive account of justice, and Kymlicka goes on to argue (2002: 75–87) that such an account is offered by Ronald Dworkin in his famous 'What is Equality?' papers and in his later book (which incorporated those papers), *Sovereign Virtue* (Dworkin 1981, 2000).

Thus, for Kymlicka, Dworkin's theory is a 'response' to problems with Rawls's articulation of an ideal responsibility-sensitive egalitarianism, and from Dworkin arises the whole industry of egalitarian theories of that kind.[13]

6.2   Rawls and equality

Kymlicka's reading of Rawls has been influential, and there are undoubtedly passages in *A Theory of Justice* that support it. Moreover, the criticisms he advances of the difference principle may stand independently of whether Rawls intended the principle to be endowment-insensitive and ambition-sensitive in the way Kymlicka thinks. However, it is possible to read Rawls in a different way. In my view, the reading advanced below fits better with Rawls's overall argument, but, more modestly, it can be advanced merely as an alternative to Kymlicka's version.[14] After all, *A Theory of Justice* is a big book, composed over a long period, and it is full to the brim with arguments, suggestions, comments, and seminal interventions into a wide range of debates.[15]

Remember, the gist of Kymlicka's tale was that Rawls claims that differences in social background are arbitrary from a moral point of view, and thus ought to be excluded when thinking about equality of opportunity. Then, since the genetic lottery is just as much of a lottery as the social one, natural talents and abilities, too, ought to be excluded.

Kymlicka's take on this is to say that both are arbitrary because they are not within the control of the agent, and so Rawls stands at the start of the development of responsibility-sensitive egalitarianism. But such a reading sits ill with a number of other features of Rawls's book (discussed below). Moreover, it relies on attributing to Rawls distinctions that do not themselves feature much in *A Theory of Justice*. Rawls does not refer to the distinction between choice and circumstances, or to ambition-sensitivity and endowment-insensitivity.

In chapter 2 of *A Theory of Justice*, from which Kymlicka draws much of his interpretive ammunition, Rawls states that 'the difference principle is not of course the principle of redress [that is, "the principle that undeserved inequalities call for redress; and since inequalities of birth and natural endowment are undeserved, these inequalities are somehow to be compensated for"]. It does not require society to try to even out handicaps as if all were expected to compete on a fair basis in the same race' (1971: 100–1). This is at odds with a responsibility-sensitive egalitarian reading of Rawls. That said, at other times Rawls seems to say things that bring the difference principle and the principle of redress very close. For example, he writes of 'nullif[ying] the accidents of natural endowment and the contingencies of social circumstances' (1971: 14) in relation to his conception of justice; and he does, as we have seen, refer to the 'natural lottery', and say of justice that 'there is no more reason to permit the distribution of income and wealth to be settled by the distribution of natural assets than by historical and social fortune' (1971: 74). However, it seems to me that if we accept Rawls's statement that the difference principle is not the principle of redress, then we are forced to try to understand these other claims and his overall arguments differently.

Think again of Rawls's project, which is to establish principles of distributive justice to govern the basic structure of society. In setting the scene, he is clear that the current basic structure of the USA or UK (and other countries) contains inequalities that are 'profound', 'deep', and 'pervasive'. Not only that, but these inequalities 'cannot possibly be justified by an appeal to the notions of merit or desert' (1971: 7). It is in comparing Rawls's justification for inequality with that offered by the ideas of 'merit or desert' that (I think) an alternative reading to Kymlicka's can be found.

A desert claim must have what Joel Feinberg called 'a desert basis'. That is, 'if a person is deserving of some sort of treatment, he must, necessarily, be so *in virtue* of some possessed characteristic or prior activity' (1970: 58). Consider a contentious, but not wholly implausible, conception of retributive justice: people who culpably commit wrong acts deserve punishment (the desert basis is the culpability of the offender for some criminal act). Thus, if we were to set up a system of just punishments, we would set it up so that those who commit wrong acts get what they deserve (which is punishment in proportion to their culpability and offence) and the innocent get what they deserve (which is not to be punished).

In one place in *A Theory of Justice*, Rawls says something strikingly like this (1971: 314–15; he also says quite a few other things about punishment, which I have discussed in Matravers 2000: 145–51). Indeed, he remarks that 'a propensity to commit [wrong] acts is a mark of bad character, and in a just society legal punishment will only fall upon those who display these faults' (1971: 315). This remark has struck many people (including, in the past, me) as inconsistent with the account of distributive justice offered in *A Theory of Justice*.[16] The problem is that *if* Rawls believes that we are not responsible for our natural talents and abilities (for our places in the social and genetic lotteries), then how can he legitimately condemn people to punishment for their bad characters?

If Rawls believes that we are not responsible for our natural talents and abilities, then his attitude to punishment is indeed deeply problematic. If not, then (again) what is needed is an alternative understanding of what he is committed to that better explains his approach to punishment.

One way to pursue such an alternative understanding is to try to reconstruct the simple conception of retributive justice given above as a conception of distributive justice. To do so, one needs a desert basis (analogous to the culpability and wrongdoing of the offender) and a connected account of what is deserved (analogous to the proportionate punishment the offender receives). What are putatively deserved are economic rewards such as income and wealth. But what, given the starting assumption of fundamental equality, could the desert basis be for such rewards? Rawls, at various points, canvasses a number of possibilities, including 'moral worth' and 'conscientious effort' (1971: 312ff). But, as Joel Feinberg puts it,

> distributing wages, profits, and salaries to whole classes of people as symbols of the recognition of superior talent seems inappropriate and, indeed, repugnant; for that would be to interpret the principle 'Better people deserve better things' in a manner wholly inconsistent with democratic and liberal ideas. That able people are *ipso facto* better people in any nontautologous sense is precisely what the traditional equalitarian . . . den[ies].
> (Feinberg 1970: 91–2)

Perhaps, for Rawls, it is in this sense that our differing natural talents and abilities are 'morally arbitrary' (cf. Nozick 1974: 227); that is, as facts about us, they have no moral authority in determining the shape of a just distributive scheme (Scheffler 2003: section III offers a particularly good account of this).

Moreover, even if we could make sense of a desert basis, how would it connect to the rewards of 'wages, profits, and salaries', which are determined by the market? Famous sports stars, for example, who happened to ply their trades in the 1950s did not (typically) make very much money; whereas stars with similar talents and abilities, doing similar things, in the post-television era make personal fortunes. Or, to take another example, a man who is a highly skilled shipbuilder and who can command a good salary one day can be made not just unemployed, but unemployable in the same capacity, the next day by a technological development (a machine is developed to do his job more cheaply) or by a slump in the world market for ships. The point is that *if* salary is meant to be what is deserved, reflecting a desert basis of conscientious effort or moral worth, then we would have to believe that when a person's salary varied because of the invention of a machine, then that change also reflects a variation in his moral worth (or in the conscientious effort he was making). But we do not, and should not, believe that. The connection between, say, salary and any proposed desert basis seems too shaky, which is something that Rawls (in 1971) thought 'obvious and has long been agreed to' (1971: 311).

Of course, that is not to deny that a just system may allow for inequalities, and that these may track differential talents and abilities. After all, if you are being operated on for a brain injury, you want your brain surgeon to be talented and able. Moreover, it may be true – Rawls thinks it is – that rewarding the talented and hard-working with greater income will generate benefits for all – most importantly, for the worst off. It is, of course, hard to square such a commitment with responsibility-sensitive egalitarianism. That said, it is also hard to fit with Rawls's claim that his conception of justice 'nullifies the accidents of natural endowment and the con-tingencies of social circumstances' (1971: 14), since there is every chance that the difference principle will allow inequal-ities that track these.

On the interpretation being offered here, what matters is not that inequalities are still likely to track natural talents and abilities to some degree, but rather that such inequalities have no moral significance as a *basis* for a system of justice (it is in that sense that, for example, 'the accidents of natural endow-ment' are 'nullified').[17] Scheffler sums up the argument as follows:

> What is relevant for Rawls . . . is the conjunction of two points. The first point is that the distribution of natural and social con-tingencies lacks any moral basis. The second point is that a system that allows the economic distribution to track the distribution of those contingencies too closely will compromise the status of some citizens as equals, for it will undermine their ability to satisfy the equally legitimate interest that each citizen has in developing and pursuing a rational plan of life that is

constitutive of his or her good. If Rawls is right, the conjunction of these two points gives us reason to reject the system of natural liberty, once we conceive of society as a fair system of cooperation among free and equal people. But the importance of these points neither derives from nor commits Rawls to the general ambition of neutralizing all of the distributive effects of bad brute luck. For Rawls, what is fundamental is the status of citizens as equals, and the moral arbitrariness of people's natural and social starting points is important because it helps to clarify the distributive implications of taking equal citizenship seriously. (Scheffler 2003: 26)

I have spent time on Rawls not just because I think *A Theory of Justice* offers intellectual resources that would be lost were it to be swallowed by responsibility-sensitive egalitarianism, but also because I think the alternative analysis offers a way forward when thinking about responsibility within justice. If a liberal, egalitarian account of justice is both to find a place for, and illuminate, the idea of responsibility, then it must face much more directly the question of what is, and what is the value of, egalitarian justice.

7   The Value of Egalitarian Justice and the Role of Responsibility

According to Scheffler, liberal political philosophy has taken a wrong turn in pursuing the currency of egalitarian justice and responsibility-sensitive egalitarianism. What has led to this, Scheffler thinks, is a misunderstanding of the value of egalitarianism. Egalitarians are concerned with the principles of distributive justice appropriate for societies of equals. Many egalitarians, including those who have contributed the most to the responsibility-sensitive egalitarian debate, take this to mean that people must be equal in some respect – in their resources, welfare, opportunities for advancement, or in some other measure. This is an understandable interpretation: equality is a relational concept. Two people stand in a relation of equality if they have equal amounts of some good. However, Scheffler thinks that there is an alternative understanding of the idea of a society of equals. 'Equality', as Scheffler understands it, 'is an ideal that governs the terms on which independently existing human relationships should be conducted.' It is not, on this understanding, 'the "relationship" of two people's having the same amount of something' (2005: 28, n. 26).

In contrasting equality as a relational concept and as a social ideal, Scheffler points to something important, but these need not be seen as opposing views of the nature and value of egalitarian liberalism. Instead, we can think of them as relevant to different parts of the egalitarian project. In what follows, I offer a brief reconstruction of the egalitarian project in which equality is both relational and a social ideal. The purpose of so doing is to try to define the space occupied in egalitarian theories of justice by questions of responsibility.

Throughout this book we have been concerned with theories that endorse the fundamental equality of human beings. If we add to this by borrowing from the account of Rawls given above and insist that natural and social contingencies have no authority in the construction of justice, then we are left with a starting point in which we affirm the fundamental equal moral status of human beings (independent of their talents, abilities, and so on). This can usefully be thought of as an egalitarian *distributive* claim: the basic idea is that of according something – in this case moral status – to some persons. The egalitarian claim is that this status is properly due to everyone – or, at least, everyone who meets some minimal capacity requirements – equally.[18]

On one understanding of this, the capacity requirements referred to above are precisely the capacities for self-reflective reason following that underpin compatibilist theories of responsibility. If so, it might be thought that responsibility is built into the very foundations of liberal egalitarianism. As already noted, egalitarians do not agree about the nature of the fundamental equality they invoke, so not all will agree that equal moral status is dependent on, or gained in virtue of, agents' capacities for reason following. However, even if it is granted that the idea of human beings as self-conscious and with the capacity to guide their actions in accordance with reasons is at the heart of the idea of fundamental equality, this does not dictate the shape of our practices of social and distributive justice. Rather, it explains why we are so concerned with the place of responsibility in those practices. Adult human beings are the kinds of things – unlike dogs, stones, and children – about which questions of responsibility can sensibly be asked.

At the heart of egalitarian justice, then, lies the distributive claim that all adult human beings are entitled to equal moral status. If so, when Scheffler appeals to the sense of equality as 'an ideal that governs the terms on which independently existing human relationships should be conducted', we can think of the fundamental distributive equality as describing the independent relationship that is then to be governed by equality as a social ideal.

How does thinking of egalitarian justice in this way help? To answer this, consider an example. On the account given above, fundamental equality of moral status is affirmed as a basic distributive principle. The question then is, What is the right way to organize a society of people who enjoy such fundamental, equal status? Take first the distribution of political rights and basic liberties. How should such rights be distributed amongst people who are fundamental equals? The obvious answer is 'equally', and that, of course, is what is demanded by Rawls's first principle: 'Each person is to have an equal right to the most extensive total system of equal basic liberties compatible with a similar system of liberty for all' (1971: 302).

However, this needs to be unpacked very carefully. The equality of persons does *not* inhere in their possession of equal basic liberties and political rights. Rather, what is being claimed is that the only appropriate principle to govern the relationship of equal beings with respect to basic liberties and political rights is one which distributes these equally. It is an *expression* of their equality, it is not that in which their equality *inheres*.[19] Once we think of the first principle in this way, it is clear that the answer 'equally' is not straightforwardly entailed by the fundamental equal status of human beings, for there may be a number of ways of appropriately expressing that status.

At first glance, this may seem paradoxical. If people are fundamentally equal, then it might be thought that it does follow straightforwardly that they must have equal political rights and basic liberties. But that is to confuse what Ronald Dworkin once usefully described as treating people as equals with treating people equally (Dworkin 1977: 227). The distribution of political rights and basic liberties must treat people as equals – in the language used here, it must reflect the fundamental equal status of human beings – but it is a separate question whether the only way to do that is to treat people equally.

Of course, in the distribution of basic liberties the case for an equal distribution as the only one that can reflect equal status may be unanswerable. In terms of political rights, that may hold, too, for the basic rights associated with the franchise. Beyond that, quite how political institutions should be arranged, the roles given to democratic decision making and to constitutional protections against majority decisions, the electoral system, and so on are complex matters.[20] Moreover, deciding the shape of political institutions will inevitably and properly involve questions of efficiency and practicality.

Liberal egalitarian citizens, then, stand in a certain relationship to one another – a relationship of equality – and what is demanded by that relationship are certain principles to regulate the distribution of those benefits and burdens that are governed by the basic structure. For Rawls, in the case of basic liberties and political rights – but not in the case of social and economic goods, which are covered by the second principle – the appropriate principle delivers equality of holdings. If we turn our attention to social and economic goods, can a similar analysis help in deciding the place of issues of responsibility in distributive justice?

7.1   *Fundamental equality and the design of social and economic institutions*

The argument above, concerning the equal moral status of human beings, can be used negatively to rule out certain understandings of economic justice. Specifically, what is excluded is a conception of economic justice in which the institutions of the basic structure are designed to reward or penalize people in order to reflect the different value of persons. That is, the idea would be that prior to the establishment of principles of distributive justice, there are morally worthy and morally unworthy people, and the proper principles of distributive justice will be such that the outcome of their operation is that the morally worthy and unworthy will receive their just rewards (each in proportion to their worth). This is the interpretation of 'better people deserve better things' that Feinberg attacks as repugnant. Social and economic institutions must reflect the equal value of persons.

That said, the disputes between liberal egalitarians, and between them and their critics, do not normally hinge on different commitments regarding the fundamental value of persons. Plato and Nietzsche (as mentioned before) thought that people were of different kinds and that, therefore, social institutions ought to reflect those differences, but few critics of liberal egalitarianism follow them. Within the liberal camp, of course, the starting point of equality is granted. In both cases, what is critical is not the idea of basic equality, but the issue of what principles respect people as equals. In particular, the focus of this book is over the place of a principle of responsibility in governing the distribution of social and economic goods.

In order to show how thinking of justice in the way I have suggested might help when approaching questions of responsibility, consider again two arguments over responsibility in their most basic form.

(A) The principles of social and economic justice that properly reflect the fundamental equal value of persons are responsibility-sensitive. That is to say, from some equal starting point, persons ought to be entitled to the products of their own voluntary choices and actions, and they ought to be compensated for the effects of chance. These principles respect the equal value of human beings as responsible agents in the sense that they are capable of self-consciously guiding their behaviour in accordance with reasons.

(B) Argument (A) ignores the ways in which agents' current choices and actions are the product of unchosen backgrounds, and the ways in which the contexts in which agents make their choices are beyond their control. In short, human beings are not responsible in a sufficiently robust sense to justify the principle of responsibility as a principle of justice. The principles of social and economic justice ought, then, to be indifferent to questions of responsibility.

Part of the point of this book is to suggest that we should not approach this dispute as one that will be resolved only when we have the proper theory of responsibility. It seems to me that there is a great deal to be said for both positions and that, for reasons given in chapter 2, the issue is best thought of as a dispute about what we want from our practices of distributive justice. That is, argument (A) is best thought of as asserting that it is only fair, for example, that people get what they have worked hard to produce. In turn, argument (B) counters that, once we understand how the economic system works and how our social backgrounds influence our characters, it is not necessarily fair (and may not be possible) for people to get what they have worked hard to produce. If we look at it in this way, then we should be reminded of the strategy recommended at the end of chapter 2. Here, we have practices of justice, ideas of responsibility, and understandings of fairness interacting. We need to consider how to put them together without thinking that there is a unique answer dictated by the 'true' account of responsibility. One thing that might recommend such a strategy is to find that it is what we actually do, and to see that, I want to turn one last time to the dispute between Dworkin and Cohen.

8   Fairness-threatening Chance and Non-fairness-threatening Chance

Recall that in addition to asking what happens if we change the story of how Louis came to have his tastes, Cohen also offered the 'expensiveness argument' as an objection to Dworkin's cut. This is the argument that it is bad luck that the objects of Louis's desires are expensive (since it is a matter of climate, other people's choices, and so on). In his response, Dworkin argues that it is an error to suppose that 'other people's tastes and preferences are matters of the *kind* of luck that can relieve us of consequential responsibility [that is, responsibility for the benefits or costs of something] for our acts or circumstances' (Dworkin 2000: 298, emphasis original). This is important, because it introduces the idea that the choice/chance distinction is not all there is to judgements of responsibility, because there are different *kinds* of chance, some of them relevant to judgements of responsibility, and others not. But what kinds of chance are there?

As it happens, Dworkin is famous for a distinction between two types of luck: 'option' and 'brute' (see Dworkin 2000: 73–4). This distinction is meant to capture the difference between luck that arises from deliberate gambles and luck that does not. Thus, if I am hit by a freak crack of lightning when I am not taking any risks – I am not, for example, continuing to play golf after the storm warning has sounded – then I suffer bad brute luck. If I invest in the stock market and my shares go up in value because of unrelated reasons of investor confidence, then I enjoy good option luck. Similarly, if more controversially, Dworkin thinks that a heavy smoker who develops cancer may have bad option luck, whereas someone who does not engage in such risky behaviour, but still develops cancer, suffers bad brute luck (2000: 74).

Whilst the distinction between brute and option luck is important, it is clearly not the one doing the work in Dworkin's response to the expensiveness argument or in his attributing responsibility to persons for their personalities.[21] Rather, what is doing the work is a distinction between what might be called fairness-threatening chance and non-fairness-threatening chance.

Consider the difference between George and Jim. George is struck down with motor neurone disease at the age of 50, whereas Jim's mental and physical abilities remain relatively sound into his eighties.[22] It is natural (and right) to say that George suffers from bad luck, Jim from good luck. Yet, this is not the kind of luck that just by itself is relevant to fairness. Why not? After all, George and those who love him may rail against the world or against providence about the unfairness of his disease. However, this really only makes sense either metaphorically or if one believes in a divine will that could have altered the position. The critical issue seems to be whether some possible alternative set of arrangements could have altered the outcome for George.

Moreover, it is only if we can make sense of the distinction between fairness-threatening chance and non-fairness-threatening chance that we can unpack our responses to the following type of example. Consider two football teams, X and Y, approaching a vital match against one another. Just prior to the match, the best player in team X stumbles while getting his breakfast and sprains his ankle, thus putting him out of the game. Meanwhile, the referee for the game has accepted a bribe from a betting syndicate to ensure one side wins. As it makes no difference to the scam which of the sides it is that eventually wins, the betting syndicate toss a coin prior to their meeting with the referee and on that basis tell the referee to ensure that it is team Y that wins.

Team X suffer from a great deal of bad luck. In particular, they are unlucky in losing their star player to a freak accident, and they are unlucky in having a corrupt referee officiating at this critical match. The first of these incidents of bad luck, though, is not fairness-threatening in any relevant sense. It is part of the game of football that the timetable is set and that the best side that can be fielded on the day is the one that must play. One would have to be some kind of choice/chance zealot to believe that the match should be postponed until the player's ankle has recovered. Thus, although there is some feasible alternative set of arrangements that could mitigate this bad luck, there is no reason to invoke it. Team X, in having its star player injure himself, suffers bad luck but not unfairness. By contrast, and whatever else is wrong with corrupt refereeing, team X suffers from bad luck that renders them in an unfair position in having a corrupt referee officiate at the match. This is the *kind* of luck that does relieve the team of responsibility for losing the game (and so the costs of losing the game ought not to be borne by team X, but rather there should be a rematch with an honest referee).

Clearly, there is an overlap between the distinction between fairness-threatening chance and non-fairness-threatening chance and that between option and brute luck, but the distinctions are not the same. We may very well feel that someone who deliberately gambles his pension on the lottery is unlucky when he does not win, but that he is not treated unfairly in being made to bear the losses. His bad luck is of a non-fairness-threatening kind. If that is how we feel, then it is clear that we think that not all chance is fairness-threatening.

The distinction between fairness-threatening chance and non-fairness-threatening chance is an important one. But it cannot help if it is understood as simply another version of the cut between things for which we are responsible and things for which we are not. If it were to be deployed in that way, it would be no less liable to the regression problem than any of the other proposed cuts. If regression is a problem, then it is so because we believe that *all* chance is fairness-threatening, at least in the sense that the fact that people's backgrounds extend back far beyond their births undermines our conviction that sometimes it is fair for people to suffer or benefit from their current actions.

In addition, remember that the choice/chance distinction was introduced in order to resolve a question of distributive justice. Now, consider the position: the question is, What is properly due to people (what is it fair that they receive)? The initial answer is that it is fair for people to benefit or suffer as a result of their choices, but not fair that they should benefit or suffer because of chance. However, that distinction cuts too deeply and (possibly) too widely. But the distinction between fairness-threatening chance and non-fairness-threatening chance if deployed in the way the choice/chance distinction was deployed results in our going round in a circle: what it is fair for people to receive is (at least in part) what results from those people's non-fairness-threatening chance.

9   Responsibility within Distributive Justice

Instead of thinking of the distinction between fairness-threatening chance and non-fairness-threatening chance as an alternative to the choice/chance distinction in deciding questions of responsibility, we should think of it as another element in our overall assessment of our practices of distributive justice. If we do that, then we are finally in a position to address the question of the role of responsibility within distributive justice.

What I have suggested underpins liberal egalitarianism is a combination of a commitment to the fundamental equal moral status of humans and the claim that human beings' natural talents, abilities, handicaps, and so on have no authority in the construction of systems of distributive justice. It might be thought that this leaves little space for considerations of responsibility, and in one important sense this is right.

Consider, again, the example of the brain surgeon mentioned earlier. Brain surgeons earn a great deal of money. One way of understanding the justice of this is to say that brain surgeons deserve what they earn because they are cleverer and more hard-working than other people, and that it is *because* they are responsible for their cleverness and ability to work hard that they deserve their salaries. One way of responding to this is to say that 'cleverness' and 'the ability to work hard' are inherited traits for which individuals cannot claim responsibility. But as we have seen, doing this only delivers the debate into the morass of the problem of responsibility.

A different, and I think more productive, way of responding is to assert that the facts of 'cleverness' and 'ability to work hard' have no authority in the construction of the system of distributive justice. Indeed, to design the system of justice to reflect unequal claims would be to deny the fundamental equality of persons. This is what may be taken as denying any place at all for responsibility in distributive justice.

That, however, would be a mistake. As I noted earlier, we want clever and talented people to be brain surgeons. In order to ensure that enough of such people choose to endure the gruelling training required to become a brain surgeon, the system will have to offer incentives such as a salary that is more than they could earn in an alternative, less demanding profession. But that is to say that the reason why we pay brain surgeons a great deal is because we need brain surgeons, and that need is a proper consideration in constructing a system of distributive justice. Once such a system is in place, we can also say that those people who become brain surgeons – who are clever and work hard – are entitled to the rewards that they get, for they have done what the system advertises will be rewarded (this is an important claim in Rawls 1971: 313ff). It is in this sense, and in a sense pursued below, that this understanding of liberal egalitarianism remains *liberal*. If the system of distributive justice contains justified positions of advantage (which is an issue discussed below), then those who achieve those positions by doing what is required are entitled to the advantages that they accrue.

Thinking of things in this way throws up two interesting results. The first is a negative one. It allows liberal egalitarians to respond to 'criticisms of economic egalitarianism that themselves appeal to the principle of responsibility' (Scheffler 2005: 7). This is surely very important. As we have seen, critics of liberal egalitarian policies often appeal to desert and responsibility and to the idea that 'better people deserve better things'. The liberal egalitarian response ought to be to push the critic to discover whether what he really means is that people are of different value and that the system ought to reflect that difference. If so, then the critic and the liberal egalitarian start from rival premises, and the argument must take a different form from that discussed here. Few people, though, deny the fundamental equality of human beings, so it is more likely that the critic will allege that a just system of distributive justice, when all important matters are taken into account, will be more sensitive to people's choices than is contemporary liberal egalitarianism. If so, then the argument turns on what the system of distributive justice should look like overall, and this brings us to the second interesting result of looking at things in the way suggested.

Consider an extreme example: in 2004, average pay amongst the USA's top 2,000 chief executives was $5.7 million, which is 475 times the earnings of an average 'factory floor' worker in the USA. Were someone to defend this by claiming that the system appropriately rewards differential fundamental moral worth, they would have to defend not only the initial inegalitarian claim, but also the thought that the market salary tracks moral worth. Such a position seems to me to be untenable. But, as already noted, this is unlikely to be the position taken up by those who would defend such salaries. Rather, what is likely to be said – indeed, what *is* said – is that such salaries are needed to attract the right people into business, and business is important to all of us. This would seem a significant challenge to the approach being suggested here, since the case of the brain surgeon suggests that a liberal egalitarianism of the kind being defended here would have to accept the market salary for chief executives.[23]

The answer to this challenge lies in considering what kind of society, and what practices of distributive justice, properly express the equal fundamental value of human beings. I have claimed that such practices do not need to be egalitarian in outcome, but must nevertheless be compatible with fundamental equality. One way to approach this, of course, is to imagine a contract between such beings and ask what proposals would be passed (or what proposals cannot be reasonably rejected). And one likely, although not of course uncontroversial, answer is that inequalities are acceptable only in so far as the overall result benefits everyone. Moreover, justified inequalities in income and wealth must be just that, and not translate into unjustified inequalities of political power, educational advantage, or whatever. If this is the result of the contract, then it seems likely that the salaries being paid to US chief executives are unjustifiable.

The above sketch, of course, is both controversial and incomplete. My intention, though, is not to offer a justification of a particular account of distributive justice, still less to argue over whether pay of, say, $1 million, but not $5 million, is acceptable. Indeed, I do not think that questions such as this can be answered in the abstract. Things such as whether people will work for a certain amount of money, and whether society should pursue economic growth and so value business acumen highly, seem to me to be contingent matters. The best system of distributive justice for a society will depend on all sorts of things, including contingent facts about it and the world and the preferences of its members regarding things such as the trade-off between income and leisure. That is not to say that anything goes. Any liberal egalitarian system of distributive justice must respect the fundamental equal value of human beings.

Saying so little here about the shape of a proper system of distributive justice might seem to imperil the project of saying anything about responsibility in such a system. However, I do not think that this is the case. If the above account of how we should think about distributive justice is right, then questions of responsibility, understood as questions of whether we are 'really' responsible in a way that should be reflected in the system of distributive justice, are no longer central. But that is not to say that issues of responsibility will have no place in questions of how we should live together.

Our natural talents and abilities, and the products thereof, matter to us in a variety of important ways. Perhaps one of the most important is that in working on something and producing some result from it we can, if we are lucky in what we choose or are able to do, express ourselves in the world. It is for this reason that most authors, for example, care about the reviews they get and feel indignant if they feel the reviewer has treated them unfairly. Similarly, the brain surgeon who endures the gruelling training feels justifiably proud of what he has done and, as noted above, can rightly feel entitled to his rewards. Of course, not every occupation is like this, and someone whose working life is spent flipping burgers may not feel the same way about the relationship between himself and his occupation (although he may). Similarly, someone who is alienated from his talents, and who does not identify with them, will not value their manifestation in the world as expressions of who he is.

In addition, there are things about us that we value as part of our identities, which we would baulk at having described as 'handicaps' or 'disadvantages'. Our identifying with them, however, does not make us 'responsible'; rather, it alters the way in which the State and other people may interact with us in a manner consistent with expressing respect for us as persons. Finally, we remain committed to a view of ourselves as agents and to the value of our 'acting' rather than being 'acted upon' (as Berlin put it in the quotation given in chapter 2).

That these things matter to us could change, if we become completely convinced of the truth and significance of the Causal Thesis, but no such absolute change is on the horizon. However, that is not to say that we can ignore the ways in which the discoveries we are making about human behaviour affect our judgements of what is fair. If the methodological suggestion of using reflective equilibrium is sound, then we should move back and forward between how we think of ourselves and others and what we think are the purposes of the system of distributive justice.

Nevertheless, to say that we will continue to demand of our political practices that they respect us as agents is to say very little about the distribution of such things as income and wealth. What I have tried to argue above is that our claim over our natural talents has nothing much to do with the salary we earn, and our desire to be respected as choosing beings has nothing much to do with a metaphysical commitment to our possession of free will. Rather, these are matters of the kind of society in which we want to live. For liberal egalitarians, a just society will be one which leaves us free to some extent to make our own mistakes whilst not allowing our freedom to result in inequalities (of all sorts) that are inconsistent with the fundamental commitment that egalitarians have to the equality of persons. This, of course, is not to say very much about what such a society would look like; but the purpose of this book is not to offer a theory of distributive justice, but to say something about the role of responsibility within any such (liberal egalitarian) theory.

I have already noted that it is a striking feature of contemporary Anglo-American political philosophy that it treats justice as synonymous with distributive justice. Issues of retributive justice are seldom discussed. Yet, responsibility is central to all forms of justice. Comparing the ways in which it is treated in distributive and retributive justice will, I believe, be useful, and so it is with the latter that the next chapter deals.

4
Responsibility within Retributive Justice

1 *Mens Rea* and Responsibility

In entitling this chapter 'Responsibility within Retributive Justice', I do not mean to limit the discussion to what is called 'retributivism' in the literature on justifications for punishment. Rather, I am going to take retributive justice to refer to criminal justice. In so doing, I do not mean to imply that there is little to be learnt from considering responsibility within corrective justice or in tort rather than in criminal law (see, for example, Ripstein 1999). On the contrary, there is a great deal that could be learnt, but every discussion has to stop somewhere, and the points I want to make can be made most clearly, I think, by considering criminal justice and law. That said, although I will use examples from various criminal laws and jurisdictions, the arguments below are concerned primarily with justice and the role of responsibility within criminal justice. They are not concerned with the detailed examination of any particular set of laws or with doctrinal questions within the criminal law (again, except by way of example).

If the arguments of the last chapter are convincing, then responsibility has only a marginal place in thinking about the principles of distributive justice, at least in so far as these determine the shape of things like market rewards and incomes. But the same may not be thought for retributive justice. Criminal liability and punishment are, for us, intimately connected with ideas of desert and responsibility. Even Bernard Williams, who, as we have seen, believes that there is no one right way to put together the basic elements of responsibility, and in particular that responsibility is not reducible to a deep notion of voluntariness, notes in passing when considering retributive justice that 'there are purposes that are served by discriminating between actions in terms of the voluntary', and he adds, 'very importantly, they include some purposes of justice' (Williams 1993: 67).

The conviction that the criminal law and individual responsibility[1] are intimately intertwined finds support in the maxim that immediately comes to mind (if not, for everyone, in its full Latin formulation) when thinking about responsibility within the criminal law: *actus non facit reum nisi mens sit rea*, which roughly means that a person is not liable (guilty) for his acts alone, but only if he acts with a guilty mind. This formula includes what are often thought of as the two separate, essential elements of a criminal offence. The *external elements* of an offence (the *actus reus*) are typically an action (or inaction) performed in some particular circumstance. The *mental element* is the state of mind of the actor in relation to the act (or omission). So, in English law until recently the *actus reus* of rape was the having of 'sexual intercourse with a person (whether vaginal or anal) who at the time of the intercourse does not consent to it'. The *mens rea* element required the intent to have intercourse and that 'at the time [of the sexual intercourse] he [the alleged perpetrator] knows that the person does not consent to the intercourse or is reckless as to whether that person consents to it' (Ashworth 1999: 351, citing the Criminal Justice and Public Order Act 1994, §142).[2]

The principle of *mens rea* expresses a number of important values, some of which are discussed below. Perhaps its most obviously appealing feature is that it captures a moral (as well as a legal) conviction that the degree to which a person is at fault for some act depends in some important part on what the person knows or intends (and that the degree of fault is related to this). As Antony Duff puts it,

As in the criminal law, so with morality. If I give you false information you can properly criticize me only if my action was at least negligent. If I mislead you negligently, through failing to notice or guard against the risk that what I say is false, I am to some degree culpable: but my offence is surely worse if I mislead you recklessly, by telling you what I know might well be false; and I am yet more seriously culpable if I intentionally or knowingly deceive you, by saying what is designed to deceive you or what I know will deceive you. (Duff 1990: 10)

This is appealing because it reflects the thought that is now familiar from the preceding chapters that our moral judgements of ourselves or others, and determinations of what we and they deserve, ought not to depend on luck but on our and their choices. This thought travels from morality to the criminal law. In particular, the intuition that punishment should track desert is very strong in most people – certainly stronger than in the distributive case. Moreover, in the case of retributive justice, many people have the connected judgement that the State's authority to punish depends on the moral blameworthiness of the offender (so, for example, the State is not morally entitled to punish an innocent in order to reassure the public). This is perhaps linked to both the enormous power of the modern State and the immense seriousness of impositions of criminal liability and punishment. Given these, we place careful constraints on the State and require of it that its use of its powers is such that we can live our lives knowing that whether the State's awesome powers are directed at us depends on what we choose and do.

That said, as we shall see in section 3 below, these convictions have not always been so prominent in the public domain (or in penal philosophy), and indeed, their contemporary resonance may well be a result of the political rise of the 'responsible individual' described in chapter 1 (see Garland 2001). Just as we should not underestimate the effects of ideas on politics, so we should not ignore the effects that politics can have on ideas. Before considering this, however, it is worth spending a little time unpacking the various ideas that go into the conviction that retributive justice is about people who culpably do wrong getting what they deserve in proportion to their responsibility for those wrongs.

2   Justice as Giving People What They Deserve

The appeal of the principle of *mens rea* described above might suggest that the role of responsibility within retributive justice is comparatively simple, in contrast to its role in distributive justice. Recall the construction of a simple desert-based argument from chapter 3: those who commit wrong acts deserve punishment (the desert basis is the culpability of the offender for some criminal act). Thus, if we were to set up a system of just punishments, we would set it up so that those who commit wrong acts get what they deserve (which is punishment in proportion to their culpability and offence) and the innocent get what they deserve (which is not to be punished).

Much discussion in the philosophy of punishment has concentrated on criticizing this kind of retributive (in the narrow sense) argument by alleging that the second part of the formula – that wrongdoers deserve punishment (for example, fines or imprisonment) – is merely asserted, and that the connection between wrongdoing and penal hard treatment is mysterious (for an extended discussion of this criticism and the replies that retributivists have offered, see Matravers 2000: introduction and chs 2–3). However, our interest here is in the formula itself as an account of justice and, particularly, in the first part in which it is claimed that the system of retributive justice is properly constructed so as to give those who do bad acts what they deserve (whatever that is).

One reason why this appeals, I think, is that it connects to what we have seen (in chapter 2) is a familiar thought about responsibility. The idea is this: in the retributive sphere, we wish those who do bad things to get what they deserve in proportion to their bad acts. The degree of their badness, and so what they deserve, will depend on their culpability. In turn, their culpability – the degree to which they are at fault – depends on their being responsible for the act (or omission), which is a matter of whether they did the act (or failed to do it) negligently, recklessly, intentionally, voluntarily, and so on, or whether they did it unknowingly, whilst hypnotized, involuntarily, and so on. That is, as Christopher Kutz puts it, responsibility is thought of as resting 'solely on facts about agents and their relations to certain harmful (or favourable) events or states' (2002: 550).

So, to return to the example of rape: Jack has vaginal intercourse with Jane who, as a matter of fact, at the time of the intercourse does not consent to it. The law against rape is established so as to give those who rape what they deserve for their bad act. The question then is, What does Jack deserve? The answer depends on the degree of Jack's badness, which is determined by examining the facts about Jack in relation to his having intercourse with Jane. If the fact about Jack is that he genuinely and reasonably believed that Jane did consent, then we might think that he is responsible for having intercourse with Jane, but that he is not blameworthy because what he did he did unknowingly. If the fact is that he was negligent in checking whether Jane consented, or was reckless with regard to her consent, or knew that she did not consent and intentionally and voluntarily had intercourse with her, then he is responsible, and the degree of his culpability, and so what he deserves, increases as we move from negligence to intentionality.

Such a model seems to many people to be right, and my guess is that it is the one thought by most people to be that which operates at the core of the retributive sphere. Moreover, such a model offers an explanation of the number of new legal excuses that have been suggested in recent years. Recall from chapter 2, there have been (successful and unsuccessful) attempts to get the law to recognize excuses based on drug, sex, gambling, and alcohol addictions; brainwashing; battered woman and premenstrual syndromes; post-traumatic stress and genetic disorders; cultural background; and indigence (this list is slightly adapted from Golding 2005: 222). One way to think of this phenomenon is as a response to the focus on the individual's responsibility, for if *that* is the issue, then what comes into play is the question of whether a given alleged offender is *really* responsible, *really* bad. So, if Jack knew that Jane did not consent, but was in the grips of a sex addiction, then the relevant facts about Jack – or so proponents of a (perhaps partial) defence of sex addiction would have it – are not as they may at first seem, and he is less culpable.[3]

2.1   Difficulties with desert

For all of its attractions, there are a number of difficulties with the model as described above. One that I have already mentioned, that it requires us to make sense of the idea that there must be some suitable connection between culpable wrongs and penal hard treatment, I want largely to put to one side.[4] Rather, I want to focus on the idea that the design of retributive institutions should be guided by the requirement to give those who culpably commit wrongs what they deserve for those wrongs.

The first problem is that it is unclear why those who believe in the fundamental equality of human beings as the touchstone for the design of political institutions and principles of justice should not find it 'repugnant' to design retributive systems so as to distribute punishment to 'whole classes of people' in recognition of their lack of virtue, just as Feinberg thinks they should in the distributive case (Feinberg 1970: 91–2; discussed above in ch. 3, sect. 6.2–7.1). That is, it may be that vicious people who commit bad acts deserve punishment, just as a hard-working brain surgeon is entitled to a high salary, but this would be a consequence of the working of a system that had as its justification something other than the idea of establishing penalties in recognition of the different moral worth of different people (cf. Scheffler 2001: ch. 10).

Of course, for some people this provides a reason to reject, or restrict in scope, the idea of the fundamental equality of human beings. The thought might be that a propensity to do bad acts expresses a bad moral character, which differentiates its holder from good moral characters in a way that is morally relevant. If so, good and bad people are not fundamentally equal in the way that tall and short, talented and untalented, hard-working and lazy, people are.

I am not at all sure how this argument could be made to work other than through sheer assertion or with the help of some mysterious celestial mechanics. It requires us to think that there are (as it were, pre-justicially) good and bad people, and that bad people do things such as have non-consensual intercourse with others. Justice thus requires that we establish laws against rape that have penalties associated with them for the purpose of ensuring that (that subset of bad people who are) rapists get what they deserve. Such intuitions are very strong among some people in both the distributive and retributive cases.[5] Yet, the argument is liable to the same two objections levelled at it in the distributive case. First, there is the egalitarian commitment to the fundamental moral equality of persons. Even if that is rejected, there is, second, the difficulty of explaining how the things deserved (fines and prison sentences, for example) track the desert basis. Of course, if we make sense of retributive justice as we made sense of distributive justice, then there will have to be some account of how the entitlements (which in the retributive case are usually unwelcome) relate to the desert basis as established by the practices and institutions of retributive justice, but that is a different matter.

Thinking of the structure of retributive justice in these terms need not mean dispensing with the (more narrowly) retributive claim that punishment is 'of an offender for a past offence'; it merely means relocating that claim. It is an important part of our practices of criminal justice that the offender is called to account and *blamed* for his offence. However, the practices and institutions through which that happens must express the fundamental equal moral worth of all persons.

That is not a problem (although it is a complex matter how to do it); as was noted in the distributive case, expressing the equal moral worth of persons does not necessarily require giving them identical treatment.

Consider again the case of rape. The purpose of having laws against rape is primarily to protect women and men from rapists. But that protection is embodied in the *criminal* law, because it is an important part of the criminal law that it condemns wrongdoing and expresses moral censure. Each of these considerations is important, and (as already noted) giving an account of how practices of punishment (particularly those that involve 'hard treatment' like fines and imprisonment) can be justified in a way that expresses the fundamental equality of human beings is a difficult matter.

All of that said, if retributive justice in general, and punishment in particular, includes this element of blame and censure of wrongdoers for their wrongdoing (and not just in order to benefit all or maximally benefit the worst-off), then it might still be thought that responsibility is more central in retributive justice than in its distributive relation, and that the straightforward desert model described above does some work in the retributive case: those who do bad acts do deserve, one way or another, bad things (even if only censure). Moreover, the degree of badness, if any, depends on facts about the wrongdoer such as whether he acted voluntarily or involuntarily. The principle of *mens rea* captures this important insight.

I think that the first part of this thought – that punishment is about giving people what they deserve – can be accommodated within the revised scheme suggested here. Our intuitions about desert can be retained if we understand desert as entitlement (although the word, of course, fits less well in the retributive case). However, the second part of the thought – that desert is determined solely by responsibility, which in turn rests on voluntariness – is, as we have seen, much more problematic. Responsibility, conceived of as a fact about the agent's intentional or voluntary action in relation to some act or event, is sustainable only if Williams is wrong and the notion of the voluntary can be deepened (so as to provide the necessary foundations for the account of justice). But any attempt to do this is liable to regression-type problems (which, as noted above, may indeed have found expression in the drive for new excuses). That is, once pressure is put on individual responsibility as some fact about the agent, it quickly seems that agents are not *really* fully responsible at all, since they are products of their social and genetic backgrounds or handmaidens of their unchosen personalities, addictions, and afflictions.

Instead of thinking of responsibility as simply a matter of the facts about the agent, then, we must place judgements of responsibility in the contexts in which they occur. Voluntariness and intention may be the most important elements in criminal responsibility, but they are not all that there is. Judgements of responsibility take place in, and interrelate with, the contexts in which they occur. As Antony Duff puts it, 'to *be* responsible is to be . . *held* responsible by somebody within some practice' (2005: 442). Or, in Kutz's words, 'attributions of responsibility' are 'fundamentally relational' in that 'they depend upon the character of moral, legal, and social relations among the actor, the victim, and the evaluator' (2002: 550).

Even if we grant the relational character of judgements of responsibility, much of the desert model can still be maintained simply by asserting that the context of criminal responsibility is one in which the individual actor and his voluntary actions are most important. In this case, it is not that facts about the agent determine the shape of practices of justice, but that the shape of those practices directs our attention to the agent and his voluntary acts. Of course, if this is the case, then some of the worries about how much weight can be carried by a notion like voluntariness return. Before turning to those, though, it is (as I said above) worth reflecting on the fact that it is not obvious, and should not simply be taken for granted, that our practices do, and still less *must*, give a central place to the agent and his voluntary acts.

3 Responsibility in Context

In the case of our own current practices, it is worth noting that the commitment of most modern legal theorists to the maxim *actus non facit reum nisi mens sit rea* is not equally reflected in the practices of the law.[6] A minor point is that the separation of the *actus reus* and the *mens rea* elements of an offence is not always respected. Often in specifying the former, the law invokes states of mind such as 'voluntarily' or with 'justifiable force'. Far more serious for advocates of *mens rea* are the many strict liability offences – 'empirically dominant in English criminal law today' (Lacey 2002: 271)[7] – that (at least for some elements of the offence) require no proof of fault. Although the majority of these do not cover the serious core offences of the criminal law, some do. Thus, to return to the example of rape, in many jurisdictions (including all the states of the USA) there is some form of statutory rape offence (although usually not under that heading, but rather 'criminal sexual conduct with a minor' or 'sexual battery of a minor') that enables the successful prosecution of, for example, a 25-year-old man for the rape of a consenting 15-year-old girl even if the man genuinely and reasonably believed the girl to be above the legal age of consent.[8] For some, as we shall see, this is a virtue; a sign of an enlightened approach to the criminal law. Consider the following variety of views on the proper nature and purpose of the criminal law.

3.1 *Holmesian objectivism*

One model of the law has it that the sole purpose of the law is to regulate conduct and (if successful) ensure that people behave in accordance with its demands. The law punishes, where people do not obey it, for purposes of individual and general deterrence. Such a model is neatly incorporated in a view that the overall welfare of the State (and its citizens) is more important than the welfare of any particular citizen.

Such a model is, in broadest outline, advocated in Oliver Wendell Holmes Jr.'s book *The Common Law* (1881).[9]

Moreover, Holmes thought that since the law demanded conformity with certain standards of behaviour, it followed that citizens should be evaluated on their conduct, not on their states of mind.[10]

Combining these thoughts, Holmes argued for a 'reasonable man' test in place of *mens rea* requirements. Thus, for Holmes, what matters is what a reasonable man would have known or foreseen in the relevant situation. What the actual defendant knew, foresaw, intended, and so on are irrelevant even to that defendant's liability. Here, as Holmes recognizes, law and morality part company, for, on this model, an individual can rightly be punished out of proportion to his moral blameworthiness (indeed, someone who is morally blameless could properly be punished) for the general good of society.

3.2   Woottian therapy

Barbara Wootton's career and views on responsibility were briefly touched on in chapter 2. Her views changed in certain details, and the strength and nature of their presentation differed, depending on her audience (and whether she was writing as a practitioner, an academic, or a policy wonk), but it is nevertheless possible to distil a broad position that can be attributed to her. Like Holmes, she thinks *mens rea* irrelevant in the construction of criminal offences; but, unlike Holmes, her reasons lie in her faith in psychosocial interventions and in her belief that it is neither possible nor useful to distinguish between the mentally normal, responsible offender and the mentally disordered who are not responsible. As she puts it, 'if mental health and ill-health cannot be defined in objective scientific terms that are free of subjective moral judgments, it follows that we have no reliable criterion by which to distinguish the sick from the healthy mind' (1959: 227).

For Wootton, the purpose of the criminal law is to prevent anti-social behaviour, a purpose shared with Holmes; but in Wootton's case this is to be achieved by treating offenders, where possible, so as to modify their future behaviour. *Mens rea* considerations are thus relevant 'after a breach of law has been proved' because of 'the light which they throw on the likelihood of his [the offender] offending again, and upon the most hopeful way of dealing with him' (Wootton 1978: 224). For Wootton, then, responsibility is not an important issue. The criminal trial simply establishes who did what.

Where the agent's actual knowledge, intentions, mental states, and so on do matter for Wootton is in indicating how best to treat him. So, the mental state that differentiates a kleptomaniac (if there is such a state) from an ordinary shoplifter is important not because it changes the culpability of the offender (which is neither here nor there), but because the psychosocial interventions that will best reform the kleptomaniac will be different from those that will best address the shoplifter.

Both Holmes and Wootton, then, have little time for the principle of *mens rea*. Our current responses to their proposals may well be negative; we may even be repelled by them. But both were influential and respected in their time.[11] Our current views, of course, are far more centred on responsibility and *mens rea*.

3.3   Hart and the importance of choice

The English jurist (and founder of modern analytic Anglophone jurisprudence), H. L. A. Hart worked at around the same time as Wootton, and it might have been expected that his Benthamite and utilitarian sympathies would have inclined him towards the kinds of positions she espoused. However, in a series of lectures and papers, he made it clear that there would be a great loss if we followed Wootton in thinking of 'punitive and medical measures as merely different forms of social hygiene to be used according to a prognosis of their effects on the convicted person' (Hart 1968: 199).

Underlying Hart's views was a particular conception of society in which the principle of responsibility played a critical role. He gave voice to this in a lyrical passage that deserves to be quoted despite its length:

> Human society is a society of persons; and persons do not view themselves or each other merely as so many bodies moving in ways which are sometimes harmful and have to be prevented or altered. Instead persons interpret each other's movements as manifestations of intentions and choices, and these subjective factors are often more important to their social relations than the movements by which they are manifested or their effects. . . . If you strike me, the judgment that the blow was deliberate will elicit fear, indignation, anger, resentment: these are not voluntary responses; but the same judgment will enter into deliberations about my future voluntary conduct towards you and will colour all my social relations with you. Shall I be your friend or enemy? Offer soothing words? Or return the blow? All this will be different if the blow is not voluntary. This is how human nature in human society actually is. (Hart 1968: 183)

Moreover, Hart continues, this fundamental fact bears on the law, for

> if . . . it is important for the law to reflect common judgments of morality, it is surely even more important that it should in general reflect in its judgments on human conduct distinctions which not only underlie morality, but pervade the whole of our social life. This it would fail to do if it treated men merely as alterable, predictable, curable or manipulable things. (Hart 1968: 183)

Behind this invocation of social relations lie three separate claims that Hart makes for the principle of responsibility, which rest on the 'simple idea that unless a man has the capacity and a fair opportunity or chance to adjust his behaviour to the law its penalties ought not to be applied to him' (Hart 1968: 181). First, it allows us to plan our lives knowing the likelihood that we will be subject to criminal sanctions. Second, what determines our future fate is our choices. Third, the law promotes the 'prime social virtue of self-restraint'. The risk that people will not always conform is 'the price we pay for general recognition that a man's fate should depend upon his choice' (the three arguments are presented in Hart 1968: 181–2).

3.4   A liberal conception

Although Hart's defence of responsibility and excuses is set against a consequentialist account of what he calls 'the general justifying aim' of punishment (Hart 1968: 8–11), it has been (and is) very influential, and is recognizably a liberal conception of a kind with which we are now familiar. Analytical jurisprudence, spurred on by Hart, has developed in many and various ways, and there is now a vast, sophisticated literature on such things as intention and excuse. Moreover, the general decline in consequentialism – that occurred in both retributive and distributive theorizing – has meant that the kinds of claims that Hart makes for the principle of responsibility are now often presented against a Kantian rather than a utilitarian background. Thus, a familiar, if not uncontroversial, account of responsibility within retributive justice now might run as follows.

What marks adult human beings out as the kinds of beings thought to be fundamentally equal to one another is their capacity for reasoning and for being guided by reasons. The criminal law presents (at least at its core) authoritative rulings on reasons for action within a limited domain. It addresses citizens as reasoning beings and insists that, when reasoning about their acts, they should take certain things into account. Where they do not do so, the law holds them to account; it asks for, and assesses, reasons that may (or may not) excuse or justify the act. Thus, the idea of responsibility embedded in this understanding is that citizens are responsible agents in so far as they have the capacity to understand and be guided by reasons. They are responsible for the reasons that they take to be authoritative and action guiding, and where these reasons are not those allowed by law, they are responsible to the law – to the community whose law it is – in that they can be called to account for their actions.

Such an account is obviously very skeletal, and it could be filled out in a variety of ways.[12] What is clear is that, in appealing to capacities such as responsiveness to reasons, it connects with much of the recent compatibilist literature surveyed in chapter 2. That said, one needs to be careful not to think that, finally, we have arrived at an account of justice in which some (best) account of moral responsibility is used as a foundation on which to build a dependent account of justice. In a sense, both the compatibilist theories of chapter 2 and this theory of the law spring out of a far greater moral and political vision of liberal late modernity. We should expect, then, that the theories of responsibility and of justice that appeal to us will, indeed, be those that are 'ours' in the sense that they fit together within our vision of a liberal society.

This feature of the argument is, of course, apparent if one stops to consider the other models on offer above. For Holmes and Wootton, responsibility is a relational concept, and one that can only be properly understood in context. It is just that once the purposes of the law are properly understood, it turns out that individual responsibility (in the way we currently think of it) is not very important.

We should not be too quick to dismiss these views. Rather, they reflect the different ways in which the elements of responsibility and the conception we have of the purposes of our practices of justice can be combined in the process of trying to find a reflective equilibrium. As already noted, Wootton's therapeutic model might strike a current reader as reminiscent of a dystopian vision of society in which citizens are manipulated and treated until they conform with the rules. Yet, both Wootton and Hart thought of themselves (and of one another) as liberals. Both wrote (less than forty years ago) against the background assumptions that the 'old' retributive ideas of punishment were dead or dying, and that the task was to formulate a new, enlightened, criminological and jurisprudential science.[13] Hart's argument was merely that there would be a place for the principle of responsibility 'even when retributive and denunciatory ideas of punishment are dead' (Hart 1968: 183). Wootton thought this insufficiently liberal. She thought that Hart had failed to take fully on board the enlightened, post-retributive age towards which we were heading. 'Even so liberal a thinker as Professor Herbert Hart', Wootton commented in a book published in 1978, 'seems unable to get away from an obsession with the idea of punishment, which haunts his text' (1978: 224). At the time of writing the book in which that comment was made, Wootton was a member of the Government Advisory Council on the Penal System. It is extraordinary, and a salutary lesson, that only a year after its publication, Mrs Thatcher's election would completely change the political and penal landscapes in a way that makes Wootton's comment seem to belong to a different, and distant, age.[14]

Nevertheless, having warned against being too constricted in one's imagination, I want to focus on the liberal model of the criminal law (as described in the section above). What is clear in this model is that it gives primacy to notions of voluntariness and moral responsibility. The role and understanding of these notions are still relational and practice-bound, but the practice is recognizably one in which they play a central part. The correct understanding of individual responsibility, then, is not epiphenomenal: it cannot simply be read off from an understanding of the proper purposes of the criminal law. Rather, as suggested by the reflective equilibrium model, the idea of individual responsibility shapes, and is shaped by, the practice and understanding of retributive justice.

If that is so, then Duff and Kutz are right that attributions of responsibility depend on the moral, legal, and social practices in which they are embedded; but in turn, those practices reflect our understanding of responsibility, which, as we have seen, has come under pressure from our increasingly naturalistic outlook. This returns us to the kinds of questions that have haunted the last two chapters concerning how a notion of individual responsibility can be made to bear the weight needed, given the threats to its very possibility.

The challenge is this: in response to the threats to responsibility, the justice theorist appeals to the practices in which judgements of responsibility are made. The threats are meant to be defused, because the response allows that we cannot find a final, right, metaphysically defensible account of responsibility on which we can build practices of justice; but then we do not need to do so. However, now, the critic might allege, we have arrived at a practice of justice – retributive justice – in which individual responsibility has such a central role that the threats to it cannot be avoided. If individual responsibility is problematic, then so is our notion of retributive justice.

Another way to put this is as follows. On the liberal model, the offender intentionally, voluntarily, recklessly, or negligently caused harm; he is responsible for this harm in so far as he is at fault; and he deserves punishment in accordance with the harm done and the degree of fault. All of this would be undone were we to find that the offender was hypnotized, somnambulistic, acting under duress, and so on, because then the harm done would not be traceable in the right kind of way to the offender. But, the critic of the liberal model alleges, none of our acts are traceable to us in the right kind of way, because all have a causal history that extends back beyond our births.

4   Putting Responsibility Under Pressure

Criminal law theorists have, of course, been aware of the challenges of determinism and/or the Causal Thesis, but, for the most part, the response has been to dismiss threats to responsibility from these sources as resting on a confusion. Consider what I shall call 'the standard response'.

4.1   The standard response

Most of the elements of the standard response are already in place from the foregoing discussion. The criminal law addresses reasons to people who are thought of as able to grasp those reasons and put them into practice. When they do not do so, the law calls them to account; it asks for an excuse or justification.

Recall the example given in chapter 2 (sect. 2.4). Someone breaks into a mountain cabin during a snowstorm in order to avoid what he reasonably regards as a good chance of freezing to death. If called to account – asked to provide reasons for his actions – he says that his actions did not manifest a guilty will but that, rather, he was responding to the conditions. Of course, his actions were caused (both in the sense that they are explained by the conditions and in the sense that they resulted from biological processes sparked in his brain), but what matters is that the reasons that governed his actions were good ones (ones for which the law does not hold people liable).

The confusion that criminal law theorists attribute to those worried by regression, for example, is this: were a different agent to break into the cabin on a sunny day and then claim, as an excuse, that his character was formed in such a way that he is predisposed to breaking and entering, we would not be impressed. Perhaps he is right, but that is properly not an excuse recognized in law. The reasons upon which he acted were, say, that he wanted what was inside the cabin, and the fact that it belonged to someone else provided, for him, no reason for not breaking and entering. This is just the kind of thing the law condemns. As a participant in the moral and legal community – and as someone capable of acting on, and giving an account of their behaviour in terms of, reasons – the agent is properly held to account (the classic account of this is Hart 1968; the position is similar to Peter Strawson's and receives a sophisticated contemporary treatment in Wallace 1994).

The standard response is, I think, too quick, and it begs the question. It does the latter because of its structure: it asks, 'given the nature and purposes of the criminal law, when is it fair to hold someone responsible for some act?' The answer can then take the form of (very sophisticated) unpacking of existing excuses and justifications to see where and in what ways these cover new cases (again, Wallace 1994 offers an account of this type). But the assault on responsibility is more fundamental; it asks, 'is it ever fair to hold people responsible for their acts?'

The response is too quick because, even given this structure, issues of responsibility manage to evade neat categorization in our existing understanding of the law. I want to take the allegation of quickness first, using two contemporary debates over 'rotten social background' and 'personality disorders'.

4.2   Rotten social background and responsibility

Some socially concerned, perhaps paternalistic, members of the advantaged classes have probably always worried about the connections between poverty and crime and about the responsibility of indigent offenders. Moreover, such worries are exacerbated if one thinks in terms of criminal *justice* rather than just criminal *law*. How can it be part of a just system that such a (statistically) significant proportion of the State's penal sanctions fall on those who are already (in distributive terms) worst off? Such worries have increased in recent years, of course, as inequalities in wealth and income have grown greater.

I want first to put to one side a set of important issues. In so far as the law is illegitimately biased against the poor, and in so far as it is implemented in ways that are discriminatory, it is unjust. Sadly, both things are true of the criminal law and its operation in the USA and the UK, and that is to be deplored; but it is not part of this argument, which concerns how the law ought to be.[15]

What difference does rotten social background make? Well, one difference is that our responses to offenders change if we find that they have been subject to deprivation as children and young adults. This is true even in the case of people who have committed terrible offences. An example is given in Gary Watson's paper 'Responsibility and the Limits of Evil: Reflections on a Strawsonian Theme' (1987). The example is Robert Harris, who brutally murdered two 16-year-old boys before eating their take-away lunches and musing on what fun it would be to pretend to be a police officer and to go and inform the victims' families of what had happened. Reading the description of Harris's crimes, one feels the full range of appropriate reactive attitudes.

A few pages later, again in great detail, Watson reports Harris's upbringing at the hands of abusive, alcoholic parents and describes Harris's spells inside various penal institutions where he continued to be abused and was raped. Reading this, one's reactions change. As Watson notes, one does not think it *inevitable* that someone with Harris's background should end up doing what he did. The thought, as Watson puts it, is not so much 'it had to be', but 'no wonder!' (Watson 2004: 243).[16] The issue, though, is what difference should this make?

One answer is that it depends on what are the continuing effects of the person's upbringing. Remember, the liberal model of retributive justice we are discussing has it that the law addresses its citizens as people able to grasp and apply reasons. Thus, unless past deprivation can be shown to have a continuing effect on the agent's capacity to do this, it is irrelevant to judgements of responsibility (an excellent defence of this position can be found in Morse 2000). This, recall, was Wallace's account of our response to deprivation (discussed briefly in chapter 2). For Wallace, the change in our reaction towards offenders that occurs when we hear of their deprived pasts is to be explained by a background assumption that a deprived past inhibits the development of an individual's capacity for reflective self-control.

As I argued in chapter 2, this does not seem to capture everything about our response to such offenders. We worry that it is *unfair* to hold such people fully responsible even if they possess the capacity to be guided by reasons. Of course, we have to be careful in unpacking that claim of unfairness. It might be – it ought to be – that we think it unfair that anyone should have such a deprived background in a modern, advanced, affluent society. That thought might give rise to a second: that it is unfair *for us* to sit in judgement on someone who has been wronged by a system from which we have benefited (this is an argument that has been pursued by Antony Duff (1986: ch. 10; 2001; 2003; 2005: 109–11) or perhaps, more dramatically, that it is impossible to do retributive justice in a distributively unjust world. These thoughts, whilst interesting and proper, are not what is at stake here (some will be pursued further in the final section). Rather, what is at stake is whether a deprived background can make any difference to responsibility even when the agent's capacities for reason following seem to remain intact.

One way in which it might is demonstrated by an example from Stephen Morse (who in turn attributes it to an audience member at a seminar):

> Imagine an eighteen-year-old male gang member who was brought up in a disorganized, broken family living in a dirty, dangerous, disorganized, deprived community. Assume that the gang member is of average or below-average intelligence and does not have much education, but he is not cognitively disabled. Perhaps he is even functionally illiterate. From his pre-teen days, family, school, and church life had little emotional hold on him, but the gang in his neighborhood recruited him. The gang offered him the sense of identity, belonging, structure, meaning and self-worth that his family and community failed to provide. Starting at an age when he was not a fully responsible moral agent – say, as early as ten or eleven – the gang encouraged him with its emotional leverage and perhaps threats to engage in various forms of anti-social conduct. He complied, and by age eighteen, he is a hard guy whose allegiance is firmly to the gang. Now, the gang asks him to execute a rival gang member. The gang no longer needs to threaten him or in any other way to manipulate him. He is committed to the gang and its projects, and he carries out the request, perhaps even proudly. (Morse 2000: 148)

For Morse, this character is not responsible (in theory, although Morse has grave doubts about the practicability of any such defence) if his enculturation is such that he lacks the capacity to understand that there is any moral issue in killing the rival. If so, then he cannot 'grasp' moral reasons, and so he lacks the capacity central to the system's requirement for being a responsible agent (this is broadly in line with Wallace's response).

That this example is not fanciful is an indictment of the societies under discussion, and again, it is important to separate thoughts about the unfairness of the system from those about the unfairness of holding this person responsible for this act. For Morse and Wallace to be right, what must be accepted is their fairly rich notion of what it is to be able to grasp moral reasons.[17] Yet, the character in the example may well have a basic knowledge of right and wrong and may well believe, for example, that killing bystanders in a gang fight is wrong. It is just that he does not believe that killing *this* rival for *this* reason is wrong.

These kinds of examples, I think, illustrate the degree to which our intuitions and commitments drive Galen Strawson's carousel. There is something troublesome about holding this deprived offender fully responsible, but it cannot just be the fact that he has a past that influences his current behaviour. We all have such pasts, so if it is *that* that matters, then Strawson is right, and responsibility is impossible. So we struggle to find something that sets this past apart. Fortunately, the standard of capacity that an agent must reach is a social, political, and legal matter (it is not given a priori), and this provides space in which to manipulate the theory to rescue this character without consigning the rest of us to a world in which responsibility has withered away. That is not to say that the argument cannot be made to work; it is just to ask whether the work it is doing is concealing from us the need for a more fundamental rethink of our practices of justice and/or our intuitions about fairness.

4.3   *Personalities and personality disorders*

In July 2004, Brian Blackwell, an 18-year-old gifted student at an expensive school, killed both of his parents at their home using a claw hammer and a knife. In addition to beating them with the hammer, he stabbed his father more than thirty, and his mother more than twenty, times with the long carving knife. He then washed himself and went to see his girlfriend. Using his father's credit cards (and the thirteen he subsequently applied for in his father's name), he flew first class to the USA with his girlfriend, where they spent around £30,000 enjoying themselves. They returned to England, and Blackwell moved into his girlfriend's house, claiming that his parents were away (this was plausible, since they had an additional home abroad), and that he had lost his key to his family's home. The bodies of his parents were found three weeks or so later where he had left them in the house. Blackwell was initially charged with murder, but the prosecution accepted a guilty plea on the charge of manslaughter on the basis of diminished responsibility after five medical experts diagnosed him as suffering from Narcissistic Personality Disorder (NPD).

Blackwell's is an interesting case, in part because of the peculiarities of the English law on murder and the special defence of diminished responsibility, which exists only as a mechanism to reduce murder to manslaughter. However, interesting as these things are, they can be put to one side for present purposes. What matters here is how we are to think of Blackwell, and how his case helps in thinking about responsibility within retributive justice. For that, we need to concentrate on Blackwell and the diagnosis of NPD.

Blackwell, it seems, lied consistently. In particular, he bragged about being on the verge of a career as an international tennis star. He used money his parents had put in trust for his education to buy his girlfriend a car, and he took her with him to test-drive an expensive Mercedes, which he later falsely told her that he had bought. It is thought that what triggered his attack on his parents was their challenging him over his spending. According to the American Psychiatric Association's *Diagnostic and Statistical Manual of Mental Disorders* (*DSM*), NPD is 'a pervasive pattern of grandiosity (in fantasy or behavior), need for admiration, and lack of empathy' (2000: 714). It is indicated by the individual's possession of five or more of the following: a grandiose sense of self-importance, preoccupation with fantasies of unlimited success, belief that one is special, a need for excessive admiration, unreasonable expectations of favourable treatment, a propensity to take advantage of others, lack of empathy, enviousness of others, arrogance (American Psychiatric Association 2000: 717). Like all personality disorders, it is controversial. To some extent, most people like to be praised, like to think of themselves as special, and like to spend time wondering (if not fantasizing) about success. As is recognized even in the *DSM*, 'many highly successful individuals display personality traits that might be considered narcissistic'. What marks out NPD is that these traits persist and are 'inflexible, maladaptive . . . and cause significant functional impairment or subjective distress' (2000: 717).

Such an example is grist to Wootton's mill. NPD is controversial, not least because it seems to some people to be simply an exaggeration of fairly standard personality traits exhibited by many people. Put one way, Blackwell killed his parents for money, so that he could impress his girlfriend. Plenty of people have killed for money, showing just as much disregard for their victims. These people are considered bad and punished. Yet Blackwell, who is not insane and does not have an 'illness' in the ordinary sense, was partially relieved of responsibility because his personality was classified as 'disordered' rather than as 'bad'. In the continuum from an ordered mind to one with an exaggerated sense of self-importance to one with NPD, there are not going to be clear lines. As Wootton would have put it, we should accept that what matters about Blackwell is that psychiatrists agree that there is no treatment for NPD. This should inform our decision about what to do with him. A killer without NPD does not differ from Blackwell in being more or less responsible, but only in being likely to be more receptive to treatment.

The assumption, though, is that we operate in the liberal (rather than in the Woottonian) model of the criminal law. The question is whether Blackwell's case, and others like it, put pressure on the idea of responsibility and its role within (the liberal model of) retributive justice.

The issues in this case are remarkably like those in the case of the gang member just discussed. On the face of it,

Blackwell is capable of reasoning and of guiding his behaviour by what he judges to be the best reasons. After all, he may not have planned the murders – they may have been impetuous – but he knew not to hang around, and he knew how to mislead people so that his parents would not be missed. We may think him – we ought to think him – mistaken in his reasoning, but that is another matter. What is it, then, that distinguishes Blackwell from an ordinary offender who kills for money?

One answer, which is that given in the case of the gang member, is that Blackwell is not fully responsible only if he does not have a proper grasp of moral reasons. This is in part an empirical matter, and the research on people with personality disorders is still in its early stages, but it is also a political and legal matter. That is to say, the issue raised by people like Blackwell should not be thought of as one that will be resolved when we have finally worked out the metaphysics of responsibility and what it is to be 'really' responsible. Rather, we should work, as is suggested by the method of reflective equilibrium, between our uncertain judgements of responsibility and the demands that we make (and that are made of us) by our practices of justice.

This method gains further support, I think, if we consider a different case: that of Byrne. Simister and Sullivan summarize the case and finding as follows:

> D [the defendant] was described by expert witnesses as a dangerous sexual psychopath, responsible for a number of atrocious, sexually-motivated killings of young women. The evidence was that the particular sexual drives of D were much harder for him to suppress and control than sexual urges of a normal character. Quashing his conviction for murder, the court ruled that his capacity to exercise self-control was relevant to his responsibility for his acts. It was conceded that the degree of difficulty that D experienced in controlling himself was a matter which fell beyond scientific demonstration. (Simester and Sullivan 2003: 585)

What is interesting about this is that it gives as the test the degree of difficulty the person has in conforming to the law's requirements (rather than in understanding or grasping them). This is clearly *not* an exact science, and indeed, the court's ruling was that juries would have to decide whether a defendant lacked full responsibility 'in a "common sense way", taking into account not only the medical evidence but also the acts and statements of the accused, his demeanour, and any other relevant material' (Simester and Sullivan 2003: 585).

Putting to one side the issues that make diminished responsibility a controversial defence, the thoughts underpinning these cases are interesting. We have laws to prevent wrongs and to hold people to account when they happen. However, not all wrongs are criminal, and not all criminal wrongs are done by culpable agents. In the cases above, the wrongs clearly are criminal, and their perpetrators are, on the face of it, culpable. Killing for money, or for sexual gratification, is just the kind of thing with which the criminal law is there to deal. The perpetrators are not children, mental incompetents, or insane. As we would normally understand it, then, the law expresses, and gives authority to, the claim that killing is (in these circumstances) wrong and demands that people conform by resisting the temptation to kill even when they desire to do so. However, some people are more tempted than others, and of those who are tempted, some find it much harder to resist.

The trouble is that all sorts of people find all sorts of things hard to resist, and yet the fact that something is hard to resist and that a person does not resist it is not the same as the fact that it is irresistible. What is happening here is that the law is making space for a common-sense judgement that even among people who have the bare capabilities necessary for criminal responsibility (the capacity to grasp and be guided by reasons) there are, as the expression has it, 'cases and cases'. It seems unfair to treat Byrne just the same as someone whose drives and motivations are less pressing, yet it may well be that, asked to account for his actions, the motivating reason for him was 'I really really wanted to', which is hardly a normal defence (and, looked at differently, makes him a rather worse person than someone who only 'really wants to' commit rape).

Perhaps, given the difficulty of research into the practical reasoning of those with personality disorders, and given the epistemic difficulties there would be were the law to call for any fine-grained distinctions, the best we can do is leave judgements of responsibility in these kinds of cases to the 'common sense' of juries. We should be aware, though, how far we have moved from the conviction that a practice-independent conception of responsibility plays a foundational role within retributive justice. It is undoubtedly important – and in more ordinary cases, questions of voluntariness and intention will be both simpler and more central to the results – but it, too, is malleable as we find that it is not straightforward, and that our convictions about when it is fair to hold someone responsible for something do not always tally with our compatibilist commitments.

5   Chance and Retributive Justice

The arguments of the above two sections are meant to show why we might think that what I called 'the standard response' to incompatibilist worries is too quick. I also said above that I thought the standard response begged the question. The reason is that compatibilists respond to these worries by asking, 'Given the nature and purposes of the criminal law, when is it fair to hold someone responsible for some act?' They then, as we have seen, consider whether, for example, a proposed defence of rotten social background, or of NPD, can be accommodated (or not) in our present understanding of excuses and defences. However, those inspired by Galen Strawson may push a more fundamental question and ask, 'Is it ever fair to hold people responsible for their acts?'

Consider the following report of an investigation of aggressiveness: 'Researchers have found evidence that some people inherit a genetic make-up that makes them more prone to aggression and violence. However, the "bad behaviour gene" is activated only if people were neglected or abused as children' (Derbyshire 2004).[18] Of course, human action is altogether more complicated than that, but nevertheless what is described is part, although not all, of the story. Now consider two men, Smith and Jones, who severely beat up a third, having been only mildly provoked. Smith has the gene in question and had abusive parents. Jones may or may not have the gene, but he had loving parents, so, even if he has the gene, it is inert.

It seems natural in this case to think that Smith, and possibly Jones, was unlucky in his genetic inheritance. Smith was certainly unlucky in this respect, and doubly unlucky in having the combination of the gene and the particular trigger for that gene. Jones may have been unlucky in his genetic inheritance, but if so, then we might think that he was very lucky to have avoided Smith's fate because of his loving parents.

Smith's and Jones's lives may go very differently. Jones, having been punished for the assault, may settle into a law-abiding life. Smith, across the course of his life, may re-offend and thus break his parole conditions; he may spend increasing time in custody as a repeat offender, and may end up in preventive detention as someone irredeemably dangerous. Yet, if the appeal of the desert argument is that each gets what he deserves, then the degree to which the outcomes for Smith and Jones depend on luck should surely bother us.[19]

There is no doubt that chance plays a role in this story, and that Smith cannot be held responsible for possessing the gene in question or for his having abusive parents. We can, of course, ask of the bad luck that Smith suffers whether it is what was identified in chapter 3 as fairness-threatening? Recall, it is clearly bad luck to be stricken with motor neurone disease, but it is not fairness-threatening. For Smith's case to be similarly non-fairness-threatening, it must be that there is no alternative system under which his life goes better, given society's need to protect itself against aggressive and dangerous individuals. In some sense this may be true; society does need to protect itself, and, *ex hypothesi*, Smith is dangerous. However, it should surely give us pause when we design the systems by which we will be protected.

As was pointed out in chapter 3, the distinction between fairness-threatening and non-fairness-threatening chance cannot rescue the standard compatibilist response to the worries created by the regression problem. Instead, it points us towards thinking about our overall practices of justice. In the case of retributive justice, the need to do this might seem even more urgent than in disputes over distributive justice. Smith does not seem to *deserve* to be the person that he is, and yet his life will go very differently from Jones's because of social institutions.[20] Yet, individual responsibility matters for all the reasons Hart provided, and so it makes us equally (or, perhaps, more) uneasy to think that Smith and all those like him should be delivered into the hands of a Woottonian system of therapy. Thinking through this, I have claimed, is a matter of working back and forth between what we know about human behaviour and what we want from our political and justicial institutions.

It is worth making one final remark. It may well be that it is not unfair that Smith's life goes differently from Jones's. That is not to say that it is fair. That Smith and Jones are different people with different dispositions is just a fact about the world that, like the distribution of natural talents and abilities, is neither fair nor unfair. What matters is how we respond to these facts. It is striking that, at least since Rawls, liberal egalitarians have been very concerned – as a matter of social justice applied to the distributive sphere – with those who do less well (and will do less well under any feasible system). The same people may well have views about retributive justice; they may decry the operation of the system, the pointlessness of mass incarceration, and the conditions in which prisoners are kept. But they do not (in general) think about retributive justice in terms of, for example, how well the worst-off group will be under the best system. They do not see it as an analogous demand of social justice that the system under which Smith must suffer should be designed as carefully with regard to Smith's interests as is the system under which the least well-off must suffer in the distributive realm. This is in part a matter of them not thinking very much about retributive justice at all; but it is also a matter, I would guess, of the residual appeal of desert in this sphere.

5
Responsibility and Justice

1 Philosophical

Asked to contribute to a series of short, 'dangerous thoughts', the evolutionary biologist Richard Dawkins offered the following:

> Basil Fawlty, television's hotelier from hell, was at the end of his tether when his car broke down. He seized a branch and set about thrashing the car within an inch of its life. Of course we laugh at his irrationality. Instead of beating the car, we would investigate the problem. Is the carburettor flooded? Has it run out of petrol?
>
> Why do we not react in the same way to a defective man: a murderer, say, or a rapist? Why don't we laugh at a judge who punishes a criminal, just as heartily as we laugh at Fawlty?
>
> Isn't the murderer just a machine with a defective component? Or a defective upbringing? Defective genes? Why do we vent hatred on murderers when we should regard them as faulty units that need fixing or replacing? We shall grow out of this and learn to laugh at it, just as we laugh at Fawlty. (*Daily Telegraph*, 3 January 2006)

I have tried to take this kind of thought seriously in this book whilst at the same time maintaining that it misunderstands the way in which responsibility functions within distributive and retributive justice. The sense in which it is taken seriously is this: it seems to me to be true that our practices of holding people responsible become more and more problematic the more we find out about the ways in which human beings fit into the world. Dawkins may express the thought in an extreme form, but it is not an unrecognizable thought, and it seems to me to be a mistake to deny its importance.

At the same time, Dawkins's approach – like Wootton's – is troublesome for a liberal thinker, because it seems to deny any space for recognizing people as thinking, doing *agents*. We do hold ourselves and others responsible, and our practices of so doing are central to our lives together. Of course, compatibilists inspired by Peter, but not Galen, Strawson will think that Dawkins is simply confused. Look, they will say, the point is that we can have our practices of holding responsible – precisely the things that seem so valuable in the quotations from Berlin (in chapter 2) and Hart (in chapter 4) – within a naturalistic view that accepts the Causal Thesis, because responsibility inheres in the very practices that Dawkins wrongly claims are threatened.

I have tried to take this compatibilist response seriously as well. Indeed, I share with it the sense that Dawkins is making a similar mistake to those he criticizes. That is to say, Dawkins seems to think that we have, in the past, wrongly thought of people as 'really', 'truly', or 'ultimately' responsible, and so we have blamed and beaten them. Once we, in his words, 'grow out of this', we will see that people are not really responsible, and so our practices must change. On both accounts, there is a foundational metaphysical commitment about the nature of responsibility from which our practices of holding responsible follow.

What I have tried to suggest in this book is that this is an unproductive way to look at the problem. Instead, we should think of our practices of holding responsible, our understandings of what it is to be responsible, and the needs we have in constructing practices and institutions of justice together. In doing so, we have to take seriously the arguments of the likes of Dawkins and Galen Strawson, but we do not need to think of them as decisive. Instead, they provide material in the search for a reflective equilibrium.

Putting things in this way, I hope, also illustrates a degree of difference between the method suggested here and the standard compatibilist response. In simply rejecting arguments like those of Dawkins and Galen Strawson as seeking the wrong kind of freedom, compatibilists risk being too complacent. By extracting a sense of responsibility from our existing practices, compatibilists may fail to see how those practices demand, if they are to be legitimate, the kind of freedom and responsibility that compatibilism cannot deliver. If so, that will conceal from us the need for a more radical overhaul of the way in which we think about these things.

Consider just as one example: responding to Cohen's criticism that people may not be responsible for their choices where those choices arise from their unchosen personalities, Dworkin dismisses the problem. 'Ordinary people', he writes, 'in their ordinary lives, take consequential responsibility for their own personalities' (Dworkin 2000: 290; for an extended discussion see Matravers 2002b). In using this to respond to Cohen, Dworkin appeals to the compatibilist insight that we should look for responsibility in our practices of holding responsible. Yet, by doing so, he not only fails to see the force of Cohen's critique; he obscures the degree to which 'ordinary people' also worry about the ways in which their personalities are formed by influences beyond their control. In short, Dworkin's complacent response may not only be misleading; in not taking seriously Cohen's worries, it forecloses what is a very important debate.

Of course, it would be over-dramatic to claim that our practices of holding people responsible are in crisis. However, there are, I think, signs that the notions of voluntariness and responsibility that can be rescued, given the naturalistic momentum of human enquiry, may not possess the kind of content needed to underpin many of the practices they are meant to sustain. That is one of the points pressed in the chapters that make up this book. The kind of enquiry recommended here, though, cannot be carried out urgently or purely by philosophical speculation. It is a matter of realizing what place considerations of responsibility have in our practices of justice, and then recognizing the need to be open to changes in both our practices and our understandings of human behaviour.

The chapters on distributive and retributive justice are attempts to illustrate what happens if one combines taking both the threat to responsibility and the compatibilist response seriously with a commitment to the fundamental equality of human beings. I realize that very little is said in both cases about what we should actually do, or about what a just society would actually look like. Instead, what is argued is that desert and responsibility do not have a foundational role; our accounts of justice will not follow straightforwardly if only we could get the metaphysics of responsibility right. At the same time, it is also not the case that if only we could sort out what justice demands, independent of questions of responsibility, then our practices of responsibility would simply be dictated by the system of justice. Rather, we have to take both together, thinking about the purposes (including, of course, moral purposes) of our practices of justice and what our understandings of responsibility will bear.

In doing this, I hope to have made a case for the connections between distributive and retributive justice and for the problematic position of issues of responsibility and desert in both. That is philosophically unsettling, but I am inclined to think that we should be unsettled, and that if we realize how difficult these things are philosophically, that should make us all the more cautious when deploying the language of responsibility and desert politically.

2   Politics

I began by reflecting on the rise of the responsible individual since the 1970s in both the USA and the UK. As indicated above, it seems to me that the language of individual responsibility that has become so politically predominant should be used very cautiously. This, of course, can be used to underpin a negative argument: one that is designed to respond to desert-based justifications of inequality.

As I noted when discussing Rawls, in *A Theory of Justice* Rawls drew attention to deep and pervasive inequalities that could not possibly be justified by appeal to desert. Although published in 1971, and so associated with the Vietnam War, *A Theory of Justice* was written in the era of the Civil Rights campaign. Much has got better since then, and the triumph of overcoming formal discrimination should not be overlooked; being a second-class citizen in terms of rights and liberties is a bad of a particular and despicable kind. Sadly, though, unequal starting points still exist in the basic structure, and recent politics, with its deployment of the rhetoric of responsibility, has attempted to justify these by appeal to responsibility and desert. The argument pursued here suggests that often that appeal is misplaced (in that it involves a denial of the equality of persons), but that even when it is understood as a claim about what could be sanctioned in a fair system of justice, it is very unlikely to be successful.

If this is true in distributive justice, I cannot see why it is not true in the retributive sphere. Questions of intent, voluntariness, and so on are of course essential to, and at the heart of, the criminal law, but they are also deeply problematic. Moreover, within a liberal egalitarian framework they must also be properly positioned: retributive justice punishes in order to uphold the equal value of citizens (which is what makes its justification so difficult). It does not punish in order to reflect in our practices their unequal value.

3 And Finally

Some time ago, when Brian Barry was the editor, an *Ethics* editorial declared that the journal would not welcome further pieces on Rawls's *A Theory of Justice* (or on abortion). It was time to move on. It is with some embarrassment, then, that having written this book I realize how often not just

Rawls, but *A Theory of Justice*, has featured in it. One, as it were autobiographical, reason is undoubtedly that part of what motivated this book was ten years of trying to explain chapter 2 of *A Theory of Justice* to students, fielding every year the same questions about why, 'if Rawls believes we are not responsible for anything, he thinks . . .'. But that is only part of the reason. The rest is that, for all the millions of words written about Rawls's project, it seems to me that it offers philosophical insights that are in danger of being lost because of the appropriation of his work by responsibility-sensitive egalitarianism. That is not to say that Rawls had it right all along, and that all we need to do is return to *A Theory of Justice*. Perhaps part of the reason for the ambiguities in Rawls's writing when it comes to responsibility is that he was aware of the risk to liberty posed by his account of equal citizenship.[1] Nevertheless, in so far as Rawls's project was motivated by a belief that it was a mistake to think that the deep and pervasive inequalities in the society that surrounded him could be justified by appeal to merit or desert (1971: 7), he was on to something that is at least as politically important now as it was then.

Notes

CHAPTER 1   THE MANY FACES OF RESPONSIBILITY

1   In so far as there is any empirical content in what follows, it will be drawn from the UK (indeed, mostly from England) and the USA. No doubt, the philosophical analysis, such as it is, could be extended to other places, but both the history to which I am going to appeal and the politics to which I will refer are fairly specific.

2   This is a complex area, as much Christian doctrine also emphasizes original sin, and there is, of course, a long history of debate about free will in the Christian tradition. That said, I think the claim above is right if understood fairly modestly. I am particularly grateful to Susan Mendus for discussion of this point.

3   Thus, for Murray, the State ought not to 'subsidize' the choice of women to become lone mothers. By doing so, it simply creates an incentive for women to act in ways that are socially sub-optimal (having a child or children in order to get a 'free handout' from the State). This argument was influential in the Republican Party in the USA during the passage of the 1996 Personal Responsibility and Work Opportunity Reconciliation Act. It has occasionally hit the headlines in the UK, but it has not had the same political influence (see Deacon 2000: 14).

4   In January 1992, Clinton left the New Hampshire Primary campaign to oversee the execution of Rickey Ray Rector. In 1981, Rector had shot and killed a police officer. He had then

shot himself. He failed to kill himself, but succeeded in inflicting severe brain damage. His understanding of what was happening when he was executed was repeatedly questioned, fuelled by a report that he had left part of his final meal to have 'later' – that is, after the execution.

5 The figures are calculated by the International Centre for Prison Studies at King's College, London. To get some perspective on these figures, the equivalent rates for France, Germany, and Italy are in the 90s. The Scandinavian countries imprison between 65 and 71 people per 100,000. Across the world, about 9 million people are in gaol, almost half of whom are held in only three countries: the USA (just over 2 million), China (just over 1.5 million), and Russia (around 0.75 million). The statistics are from the end of February 2006. See <http://www.kcl.ac.uk/depsta/rel/icps/home.html>.

6 Up-to-date information can be found at The Sentencing Project, <http://www.sentencingproject.org/>. For excellent critiques of the racial bias in US criminal justice, see Donziger 1995; Wacquant 2002.

7 On 1 March 2005, by a majority of five to four, the US Supreme Court decided (in *Roper v. Simmons*) that the execution of people for crimes committed when they were under 18 was unconstitutional. See <http://www.supremecourtus.gov/opinions/04pdf/03-633.pdf>.

8 Tracing the connections between political rhetoric and public policy is a difficult, and inexact, science. Nevertheless, it is hard not to draw some conclusions from the coincidence of the rise of the language of personal responsibility in the USA and the UK and the dramatic rise of inequalities in income and wealth that have resulted from the policies implemented in those countries. Even if one does not agree with all his conclusions and prescriptions, Brian Barry (2005) has provided a powerful argument that the language of personal responsibility has provided the cover under which governments could enrich the few at the expense of the very many.

CHAPTER 2   THINKING ABOUT RESPONSIBILITY

1 This is the conclusion that Barry comes to in his most recent book, *Why Social Justice Matters* (2005).

2 Smart's theory has recently been revisited by Richard Arneson (2003).

3 As well as an extraordinarily long career as a magistrate, spells on Government committees dealing with taxes and drugs, and (from 1958) as an active member of the House of Lords, Barbara Wootton's career involved the (Streatfield) Committee on the Business of the Criminal Courts, 1958–61; the (Perks) Committee on Criminal Statistics, 1963–7; the abortive Royal Commission on the Penal System, 1964–6; and the Advisory Council of the Penal System, 1966–77 (Wootton 1967, 1978).

4 For a critical discussion, see Wallace (1994: appendix 2).

5 Grant, arguably counter-factually, that someone brought up with a concern for social justice had reason to vote for Kerry.

6 Human beings, of course, differ in their capacities for self-conscious reason following, and these capacities change over the course of agents' lives. Agency, in liberal egalitarian morality and law, is a matter of meeting some fairly minimal threshold requirement with respect to these capacities.

7 I have borrowed the term 'mesh compatibilists' from John Martin Fischer. He first deploys it (I think) in Fischer (1987). Fischer's criticisms of mesh theories are further developed in Fischer and Ravizza (1998: 185ff.)

8 Whether he does so or not is a difficult question (and it may be that he has changed his mind). For a discussion of the issue, see Watson (2004: 303, n. 12).

9 The reason why it might not always be at that time is that we sometimes hold an agent responsible for some act (say crashing a car when drunk) even if at the time of the act the mesh did not obtain. Here, responsibility for crashing the car is traced back to the moment when the agent got drunk.

10 This argument, pursued in the following paragraph, owes a great deal to Fischer and Ravizza (1998: 196ff.).

11 Again, the name is taken from Fischer (1999: 127).

12 As Wallace notes, this account of excuses finds an early expression in Austin's 'A Plea for Excuses' (1979).

13 I have considered Wallace's application of this approach to psychopathy elsewhere (see Matravers 2005).

14 In the case of someone who, say, knowingly and wilfully gets drunk and subsequently has a motor accident, the 'current will'

and 'current capacities' will refer to the moment at which he got drunk, not the moment of the car accident. However, as noted earlier in the chapter, this does not change the basically ahistorical nature of the argument.

15 For those who find the JoJo example too stylized, think of black youths raised in depressed conditions in the ghettos and gangs of some US cities. Some may embrace the gang culture, peddle drugs, and commit serious crimes. It is surely odd to think that the *only* way to accommodate the significance of their upbringing is to think that their decisions are the result of their having impaired powers of reflective self-control. Of course, others may not embrace the gang culture, but decide that the traffic in drugs offers the only way to survive.

16 Of course there are also many other issues that revolve around deprivation and justice.

17 Here, as elsewhere, I am offering a very brief gloss on what are complex and intricate arguments. Fischer and Ravizza's book, like Wallace's, repays close study, and both offer far more insights than I can possibly mention here.

18 A possible problem arises if one imagines a group who believe that responsibility is transferable to the next of kin of the original actor. My inclination is to think that it is not the original responsibility for the act that transfers, but the responsibility for 'making up for it'. That is, the responsibility for the 'debt', but not the 'act', transfers.

19 He also kills two herdsmen, although, as Williams says, 'Sophocles makes nothing of it' (Williams 1993: 72).

20 'The concept of the voluntary is also superficial, because even if it is established that the agent's action was intentional in a normal state (e.g., highly premeditated), there is a further question of why he is someone who can want to do such things, whether it is in his control that he is such a person, and so on. It is clear that if voluntariness is to do its work such questions cannot be pressed beyond a certain point. It is not that they get a favourable answer, as free-will libertarians suppose, nor that they get an unfavourable answer which puts moral responsibility out of business. Nor again is it, as some reconcilers perhaps suppose, that there is a transparent rationale for construing the voluntary within certain limits that exclude those questions. It is simply that the voluntary is an inherently

superficial concept which should not be asked to do too much'
(Williams 1997: 101–2).

21 In his 'Voluntary Acts and Responsible Agents' (1995),
Williams explicitly connects conceptions of responsibility to
'kinds of politics'. See also Williams 1997.

22 In a sense, then, it seems to me that Strawson is right to be frus-
trated at the continuing turns taken on the carousel by those
attempting to give the right account of responsibility. However, when it comes to our moral, legal, and political practices,
the way the carousel turns has a lot to teach us.

CHAPTER 3   RESPONSIBILITY WITHIN DISTRIBUTIVE JUSTICE

1 This formulation is attributed to Justinian (see Miller 1987;
Barry 2005: 4; Barry and Matravers 2005).

2 There is no reason why this formulation should apply only to
distributive justice, but the writers examined in this chapter all
restrict their theories to the distributive realm (i.e., they do not
deal with justice in, e.g., tort or criminal law). One of the more
puzzling features of the recent literature is the way in which it
deploys the term 'justice' as almost synonymous with 'distributive justice'. Consider Jeremy Waldron, writing on 'justice' in
a volume devoted to reviewing the state of the discipline: 'what
is the present state of discussion in legal and political theory so
far as the topic of justice is concerned? By *justice*, I mean social
or distributive justice' (2002b: 266). I have argued elsewhere
(Matravers 2000) that this is not an accident, but that most
contemporary theories of distributive justice are unable to
provide plausible accounts of retributive justice, and that this
is evidence of a deep structural flaw in such theories.

3 There is the additional problem of the different political meanings of 'liberal' in the UK, where it is a fairly innocuous term,
and the USA, where it has become almost a term of abuse levelled by those on the right to describe and discredit anyone to
their left. Thus, books in the USA can carry titles like *Deliver
Us from Evil: Defeating Terrorism, Despotism, and Liberalism*,
and *Treason: Liberal Treachery from the Cold War to the War on
Terrorism*, which need translation for a British audience. To
make things still more complicated, in continental Europe, 'lib-
eralisme' often means something more like 'libertarianism'.

4 The type of liberalism – or the family of liberal theories – considered here is similar to the conception of liberalism which is the focus of Paul Kelly's (2005) wonderful, concise, account of liberalism.

5 The nature of this commitment to the fundamental equality of persons is hotly contested. Critics of liberalism often allege that liberals beg the question by assuming that persons are equal since the basic question is one about how we should think of, and treat, one another (Matravers 2000; Waldron 2002a). The main contemporary liberal writers within this tradition have offered different interpretations of their basic commitment to equality (see, e.g., Rawls 1971, esp. §87; Dworkin 1996).

6 Although this paper has been cited as 'in press' for some time (including in Anderson 1999), it is currently available only on Arneson's web-site, http://philosophy2.ucsd.edu/~rarneson/> (accessed 20 March 2005). Arneson, forthcoming: 1.

7 This example – and the issue of expensive tastes more generally – has been important in what is called the 'equality of what? debate', which in turn has been an important part of the development of responsibility-sensitive egalitarianism. The nature of the debate is over the so-called currency of justice. That is, the assumption is that (egalitarian) justice requires (at least initially) the equal distribution of something. The question is, 'What is that something?' One answer is 'welfare', another 'resources'. The debate has spawned numerous sophisticated papers and many answers as well as some severe criticisms (see Anderson 1999; Barry 2005: 22; Scheffler 2005: 20).

8 Rawls seems to have something of this sort in mind when he writes of a 'social division of responsibility' (Rawls and Freeman 1999: 371).

9 Cohen accepts this implication of his straightforward account. 'If there is no such thing' as genuine choice, he writes, 'then all differential advantage is unjust' (Cohen 1993: 28).

10 The index of *A Theory of Justice*, which is completely reliable, gives only three references for 'responsibility', the most significant of which refers to Rawls's discussion of civil disobedience.

11 Rawls himself thought of the social contract argument (of chapter 3) as the most important, but this is disputed (see Dworkin 1975; Barry 1989; Kymlicka 2002: 67–70).

12 Rawls adapted this passage in the 2nd edn in order to deflect the criticism that he thought there should be some kind of levelling out of natural talents and abilities. The revised passage reads: 'No one deserves his greater natural capacity nor merits a more favorable starting place in society. But, of course, this is no reason to ignore, much less to eliminate these distinctions. Instead, the basic structure can be arranged so that these contingencies work for the good of the least fortunate. Thus we are led to the difference principle if we wish to set up the social system so that no one gains or loses from his arbitrary place in the distribution of natural assets or in his initial position in society without giving or receiving compensating advantages in return' (Rawls 1999: 87).

13 Thus it is part of Kymlicka's story that 'much of the most interesting work on distributive justice in the last twenty years has started from Dworkin's basic premises and attempted to refine our ideas of ambition-sensitivity and endowment-insensitivity' (Kymlicka 2002: 86).

14 In writing this section, I have taken my cues from Rawls. However, I am sure that my views and their presentation have been influenced by three excellent studies of Rawls and egalitarianism by Scheffler and Mandle (Mandle 2000: 124ff; Scheffler 2003, 2005).

15 As Nagel puts it, '*A Theory of Justice* is a giant of a book; its many different lines of thought have different starting points, and if they don't all lead exactly in the same direction, that is not necessarily a defect' (1995: 122).

16 It is, says Scheffler (before he, too, changed his mind), 'an insufficiently motivated departure from [Rawls's] general attitude to desert [that is] dubiously consistent with his account of distributive justice' (2001: 18, n. 7; cf. Scheffler 2001: ch. 10).

17 Even this passage in Rawls is open to an interpretation compatible with the account being offered here. As Mandle notes, 'in the next sentence he [Rawls] suggests that the "nullification" occurs in the process of searching for the principles rather than in the principles themselves: "They [the principles] express the result of leaving aside those aspects of the social world that seem arbitrary from a moral point of view." (*TJ*, 15) Furthermore, in the revised edition, Rawls replaced the sentence with the following: "Once we decide to look for

a conception of justice that prevents the use of the accidents of natural endowment and the contingencies of social circumstance as counters in a quest for political and economic advantage, we are led to these principles" (Rawls 1999: 14)' (Mandle 2000: 132, n. 93).

18 I am grateful to John Charvet for discussion of this point. Of course, depending on how one defends the egalitarian starting point, the idea of 'distribution' here will seem more or less metaphorical. On the one hand, if fundamental equality is simply an axiom of the theory, then there is no distribution of status as such (although I think it remains a useful metaphor). On the other, one can think of equal status as accorded collectively through the social contract, in which case the idea of distribution of status has more bite.

19 It is interesting to note that Nagel, in an early paper on equality (1979), distinguished between 'communitarian' and 'individualistic' arguments for the intrinsic value of equality in a way that is similar to the distinction made here between equality as an ideal that structures relations and equality as a distributive relation. Nagel particularly associated Rawls with the distributive, individualistic model (1979: 108–9). This was consistent with his other writings on Rawls of the time. Many years later, in 1995, in a short introduction to a reprint of an early review of his of Rawls, Nagel conceded that his earlier writings on Rawls 'neglected . . . Rawls's conception of justice as fairness as a moral theory of interpersonal *relations*'. He goes on in a way that strongly suggests an interpretation of 'the moral nerve' of *A Theory of Justice* similar to the one being offered here (Nagel 1995: 122).

20 It will undoubtedly be easier to say when a system is unjust (because it clearly does not respect the equal status of persons) than to identify what is positively required by justice.

21 Of course, we could specify the examples so as to make gambles relevant. Imagine that Louis deliberately cultivated his taste for champagne because he believed that there would soon be a world glut of champagne and the price would fall. However, it does not seem to me that this would advance the issue.

22 The example is borrowed from a conversation with Brian Barry.

23 For a coruscating critique of contemporary inequalities, see Barry (2005).

CHAPTER 4   RESPONSIBILITY WITHIN RETRIBUTIVE JUSTICE

1   I shall put to one side issues of corporate criminal responsibility, although these, too, are important.

2   This was revised in the Sexual Offences Act 2003. The new legislation is more complex, and so less useful as a simple example (for a particularly useful discussion, see Simester and Sullivan 2003: ch. 12).

3   In an interesting case from tort law, Kentucky gynaecologist Harold Crall had to surrender his medical licence in 1994 after having what he called 'inappropriate contact' with some of his female patients. Although the licensing board later let him resume practising medicine, a condition was that he worked in the State Corrections Department and never saw another female patient unchaperoned. He attempted to sue his insurance company for $8,700 a month in disability benefits, claiming that his sexual addiction prevented him from pursuing his chosen profession (see <http://www.overlawyered.com/archives/99oct1.html>, accessed 23 June 2005).

4   I have said enough elsewhere (see Matravers 2000).

5   At a conference on desert, for example, Shelly Kagan responded to my inability to grasp this kind of brute claim about desert by offering the thought that Hitler was a less deserving person than Mother Teresa and that it would thus be a 'good thing' if Mother Teresa's life went better (however understood) than Hitler's (see also Kagan's contribution to Olsaretti 2003, in which the papers from the conference are published). In my view, the plausibility of this claim rests on our filling in the institutional settings in which such claims might be made. So, for example, we can make sense of the thought that Hitler (had he lived) would have deserved to be tried and punished along with his colleagues at Nuremberg and that, within the understandings of the Catholic Church, Mother Teresa deserved to be beatified. But the plausibility of these claims depends (or at least it does for me) on the plausibility of the justifications for the institutions within which the desert claims are made.

6   James Fitzjames Stephen comments on this maxim that it 'not only looks more instructive than it really is, but it suggests fallacies which it does not precisely state'. He goes on to comment, 'legal maxims in general are little more than pert

headings of chapters. They are rather minims than maxims, for they give not a particularly great but a particularly small amount of information. As often as not, the exceptions and qualifications to them are more important than the so-called rules' (Stephen 1883: 94).

7 Ashworth and Blake (1996) estimate that almost half of all English criminal offences are, or contain an element of, strict liability.

8 The situation in English criminal law is interesting. For 125 years, the leading case was *Prince* (1875). Henry Prince was charged with having unlawfully taken Annie Phillips, an unmarried girl, who was under the age of 16 years, 'out of the possession and against the will of her father'. Phillips was 14, but looked very much older than 16. She had told Prince that she was 18, and Prince (not unreasonably) believed her. Prince was convicted, the court ruling that the age of the girl was a matter of strict liability. *Prince*, in Andrew Ashworth's words, 'has been paraded by academic lawyers as the acme of injustice' (Ashworth 1999: 364). Despite this, *Prince* provided the foundation for many subsequent decisions. However, a recent case seems to have overturned it. *B v. DPP* concerned a boy of 15 who repeatedly requested oral sex from a 13-year-old girl. The boy was convicted of inciting a girl of under 14 to commit an act of gross indecency. The Youth Court ruling followed *Prince* in holding that the boy's state of mind concerning the girl's age was irrelevant. The boy appealed. Eventually, the House of Lords overturned the conviction, finding that the common law presumption of *mens rea* is 'an unexpressed ingredient of every statutory offence' unless Parliament has 'expressly or by necessary implication' indicated otherwise (Simester and Sullivan 2003: 171–2).

9 Three of the positions that follow are, like this one, identified with some particular theorist (Holmes, Wootton, and Hart). But the names operate just as 'tags' for broad-brush accounts (and each can claim far more sophistication than is evident in these quick summaries).

10 Holmes's argument here seems flawed. He claims that since the law is concerned with regulating external conduct (the things we do and do not do), it follows that the appropriate test of liability is also external. But that does not *necessarily* follow. The law can aim to regulate behaviour whilst maintaining

a concern (in particular when it comes to liability) for the internal state of mind of the particular individual.

11 Wootton's career is summarized in ch. 2, n. 3. Holmes was a distinguished American jurist, briefly a Harvard Professor of Law, and an Associate Justice of the US Supreme Court for thirty years (1902–32).

12 It is compatible, I think, with an autonomy-based view of law such as that offered by Ashworth (1999), as well as with a more communitarian, Aristotelian vision such as that offered by Duff (1986, 2001, 2005).

13 As Sue Mendus has pointed out to me, it is the idea of 'science' that is critical. For Wootton, and others like her, just as witch hunting died when it was realized that people died of heart attacks, not of curses, so punishment will die when people realize that wrongdoing is a 'disease'.

14 According to his biographer, Hart memorably described Mrs Thatcher as 'the worst head of Government since Richard III' (Lacey 2004: 357).

15 The situation in the USA (to a far greater extent than in the UK) is made worse by racial biases (for deeply depressing critiques of the US system, see Donziger 1995; Wacquant 2002).

16 Watson has reflected further on this case and on whether it reveals different faces of responsibility in a later essay (Watson 2004: ch. 9).

17 Of the kind endorsed by Wallace and Duff (see ch. 2, sect. 4.2; Duff 1977; Wallace 1994).

18 This was a summary of research done on chimpanzees, but similar findings can be found in humans (see Caspi, McClay et al. 2002).

19 In an interesting case, Stephen Mobley, who had been convicted for murder in Georgia (and was executed in 2005), tried to get genetic testing to show that he was predisposed to violence for use in mitigation in the sentencing phase of his trial. The court found that he 'was not entitled to funds for expert witnesses to conduct preliminary testing to determine whether he suffered from a deficiency of enzymatic activity for monoamine oxidase A with follow-up genetic testing to be used as evidence in mitigation in sentencing phase to suggest a possible genetic basis for violent and impulsive behavior' (*Mobley* v. *State*, 455 S.E.2d 61 (Ga. 1995)).

20 It is something like this thought that clearly underpins Scanlon's remark that 'when we criticize someone who has behaved badly, or when we follow a policy that leads to some people's being injured because they have ignored the warnings they were given, we may be correct in feeling that what we do is justified. But we must also recognize that what separates us from such people is not just, as we would like to think, that we behave better and choose more wisely, but also our luck in being the kind of people who respond in these ways. In this respect our attitude towards those who suffer or are blamed should not be "You asked for this" but rather "There but for the grace of God go I" ' (Scanlon 1998: 294).

CHAPTER 5   RESPONSIBILITY AND JUSTICE

1 This was suggested by an anonymous reader of the manuscript. The risk is real, and Kymlicka and others are right to have worried about Rawls's seeming indifference to how those in the worst-off group come to be so.

References

American Psychiatric Association (2000). *Diagnostic and Statistical Manual of Mental Disorders: DSM-IV-TR*. Washington, DC: American Psychiatric Association.

Anderson, E. S. (1999). What Is the Point of Equality? *Ethics* 109(2): 287–337.

Appiah, A. (2001). Review of R. Dworkin *Sovereign Virtue. The New York Review of Books*, 26 April.

Arneson, R. (2003). The Smart Theory of Moral Responsibility and Desert. In *Desert and Justice*, ed. S. Olsaretti, Oxford: Clarendon Press, 233–58.

Arneson, R. (forthcoming). Rawls, Responsibility, and Distributive Justice. In *Justice, Political Liberalism, and Utilitarianism: Themes from Harsanyi*, ed. M. Salles and J. A. Weymark, Cambridge: Cambridge University Press.

Ashworth, A. (1999). *Principles of Criminal Law*. Oxford: Oxford University Press.

Ashworth, A. and M. Blake (1996). The Presumption of Innocence in English Criminal Law. *Criminal Law Review*: 306–17.

Austin, J. L. (1979). A Plea for Excuses. In *Philosophical Papers*, ed. J. O. Urmson and G. Warnock, Oxford: Oxford University Press, 175–204.

Barry, B. M. (1989). *A Treatise on Social Justice*, vol. 1: *Theories of Justice*. Hemel Hempstead: Harvester-Wheatsheaf.

Barry, B. M. (1991). Chance, Choice, and Justice. In *Liberty and*

Justice: Essays in Political Theory, vol. 2, Oxford: Clarendon Press, 142–58.

Barry, B. M. (1997). The Politics of Free Will. *Tijdschrift voor Filosofie* 59: 615–30.

Barry, B. M. (2005). *Why Social Justice Matters*. Cambridge: Polity.

Barry, B. M. and M. Matravers (2005). Justice. In *The Shorter Routledge Encyclopaedia of Philosophy*, ed. E. Craig, Oxford: Routledge.

Berlin, I. (1969). *Four Essays on Liberty*. Oxford: Oxford University Press.

Burgess, A. (1962). *A Clockwork Orange*. Oxford: Heinemann.

Butler, S. (1872). *Erewhon: Or Over the Range*. London.

Caspi, A., J. McClay, et al. (2002). Role of Genotype in the Cycle of Violence in Maltreated Children. *Science* 297: 851–4.

Cohen, G. A. (1989). On the Currency of Egalitarian Justice. *Ethics* 99(4): 906–44.

Cohen, G. A. (1993). Equality of What? On Welfare, Goods, and Capabilities. In *The Quality of Life*, ed. M. Nussbaum and A. Sen, Oxford: Oxford University Press, 9–29.

Cohen, G. A. (2004). Expensive Taste Rides Again. In *Dworkin and His Critics: With Replies by Dworkin*, ed. J. Burley, Oxford: Blackwell Publishing, 3–29.

Cummins, R. (1980). Culpability and Mental Disorder. *Canadian Journal of Philosophy* 10: 207–32.

Daniels, N. (1996). *Justice and Justification: Reflective Equilibrium in Theory and Practice*. Cambridge: Cambridge University Press.

Deacon, A. (2000). Learning from the US? The Influence of American Ideas upon 'New Labour' Thinking on Welfare Reform. *Policy and Politics* 28(1): 5–18.

Derbyshire, D. (2004). Scientists Find Genetic Link to Bad Behaviour. *The Daily Telegraph*, London, 20 July 2004.

Donziger, S. A. (1995). *The Real War on Crime: The Report of the National Criminal Justice Commission*. New York: HarperCollins.

Duff, R. A. (1977). Psychopathy and Moral Understanding. *American Philosophical Quarterly* 14: 189–200.

Duff, R. A. (1986). *Trials and Punishments*. Cambridge: Cambridge University Press.

Duff, R. A. (1990). *Intention, Agency and Criminal Liability: Philosophy of Action and the Criminal Law*. Oxford: Basil Blackwell.

Duff, R. A. (2001). *Punishment, Communication, and Community.* Oxford and New York: Oxford University Press.

Duff, R. A. (2003). I Might Be Guilty, But You Can't Try Me: Estoppel and Other Bars to Trial. *Ohio State Journal of Criminal Law* 1: 245–59.

Duff, R. A. (2005). Who is Responsible, for What, to Whom? *Ohio State Journal of Criminal Law* 2(2): 441–61.

Dworkin, R. (1975). The Original Position. In *Reading Rawls: Critical Studies on Rawls'* A Theory of Justice, ed. N. Daniels, Stanford, Calif.: Stanford University Press, 16–52.

Dworkin, R. (1977). *Taking Rights Seriously.* London: Duckworth.

Dworkin, R. (1981). What is Equality? Part I: Equality of Welfare; Part II: Equality of Resources. *Philosophy and Public Affairs* 10(3/4): 185–246, 283–345.

Dworkin, R. (1996). Objectivity and Truth: You'd Better Believe It. *Philosophy and Public Affairs* 25(1): 87–139.

Dworkin, R. (2000). *Sovereign Virtue: The Theory and Practice of Equality.* Cambridge, Mass.: Harvard University Press.

Feinberg, J. (1970). *Doing & Deserving: Essays in the Theory of Responsibility.* Princeton, N.J.: Princeton University Press.

Fischer, J. M. (1987). Responsiveness and Moral Responsibility. In *Responsibility, Character, and the Emotions: New Essays in Moral Psychology,* ed. F. Schoeman, Cambridge: Cambridge University Press, 81–106.

Fischer, J. M. (1996). Review of R. Jay Wallace, *Responsibility and the Moral Sentiments. Ethics* 106(4): 850–3.

Fischer, J. M. (1999). Recent Work on Moral Responsibility. *Ethics* 110(1): 93–139.

Fischer, J. M. and M. Ravizza (1998). *Responsibility and Control: A Theory of Moral Responsibility.* Cambridge: Cambridge University Press.

Garland, D. (2001). *The Culture of Control: Crime and Social Order in Contemporary Society.* Oxford: Oxford University Press.

Golding, M. P. (2005). Responsibility. In *The Blackwell Guide to the Philosophy of Law and Legal Theory,* ed. M. P. Golding and W. A. Edmundson, Oxford: Blackwell Publishing, 221–35.

Hart, H. L. A. (1965). *The Morality of the Criminal Law: Two Lectures.* Jerusalem: Magnes Press, Hebrew University.

Hart, H. L. A. (1968). *Punishment and Responsibility: Essays in the Philosophy of Law.* Oxford: Oxford University Press.

Holmes, O. W. (1881). *The Common Law*. Boston: Little Brown and Company.

Hurley, S. L. (2003). *Justice, Luck, and Knowledge*. Cambridge, Mass.: Harvard University Press.

James, W. (1979). *The Will to Believe and Other Essays in Popular Philosophy*. Cambridge, Mass.: Harvard University Press.

Kane, R. (1999). Review of *Responsibility and Control*: A Theory of Moral Responsibility. *The Philosophical Quarterly*, 49, no. 197: 543–5.

Kelly, P. (2005). *Liberalism*. Cambridge: Polity.

Kutz, C. (2002). Responsibility. In *The Oxford Handbook of Jurisprudence & Philosophy of Law*, ed. J. Coleman and S. Shapiro, Oxford: Oxford University Press, 548–87.

Kymlicka, W. (2002). *Contemporary Political Philosophy: An Introduction*. Oxford: Oxford University Press.

Lacey, N. (2002). Legal Constructions of Crime. In *The Oxford Handbook of Criminology*, ed. M. Maguire, R. Morgan and R. Reiner, Oxford: Oxford University Press, 264–85.

Lacey, N. (2004). *A Life of H.L.A. Hart: The Nightmare and the Noble Dream*. Oxford: Oxford University Press.

Mandle, J. (2000). *What's Left of Liberalism? An Interpretation and Defense of Justice as Fairness*. Lanham, Md., and London: Lexington Books.

Matravers, M. (2000). *Justice and Punishment: The Rationale of Coercion*. Oxford: Oxford University Press.

Matravers, M. (2002a). Luck, Responsibility, and 'The Jumble of Lotteries that Constitutes Human Life'. *Imprints: A Journal of Analytical Socialism* 6(1): 28–43.

Matravers, M. (2002b). Responsibility, Luck, and the 'Equality of What?' Debate. *Political Studies* 50(3): 558–72.

Matravers, M. (2005). Psychopathie, responsabilité et théorie politique. In *Le Châtiment: Histoire, Philosophie et Partiques de la Justice Pénale*, ed. C. Nadeau and M. Vacheret, Montreal: Liber, 97–117.

Miller, D. (1987). Justice. In *The Blackwell Encyclopaedia of Political Thought*, ed. D. Miller, Oxford: Blackwell Publishers, 260–3.

Miller, D. (1999). *Principles of Social Justice*. Cambridge, Mass.: Harvard University Press.

Morse, S. J. (2000). Deprivation and Desert. In *From Social Justice to Criminal Justice: Poverty and the Administration of Criminal Law*, ed. W. C. Heffernan and J. Kleinig, New York and Oxford: Oxford University Press, 114–60.

Nagel, T. (1979). Equality. In *Mortal Questions,* Cambridge: Cambridge University Press, 106–27.

Nagel, T. (1979). Moral Luck. In *Mortal Questions,* Cambridge: Cambridge University Press, 24–38.

Nagel, T. (1995). *Other Minds: Critical Essays, 1969–1994.* New York and Oxford: Oxford University Press.

Nozick, R. (1974). *Anarchy, State and Utopia.* New York: Basic Books.

Orwell, G. (1949). *Nineteen Eighty-Four: A Novel.* London: Secker & Warburg.

Olsaretti, S. (ed.) (2003). *Desert and Justice.* Oxford: Clarendon Press.

Rawls, J. B. (1971). *A Theory of Justice.* Cambridge, Mass.: Harvard University Press; 2nd edn 1999.

Rawls, J. B. and S. R. Freeman (1999). *Collected Papers.* Cambridge, Mass., and London: Harvard University Press.

Ripstein, A. (1999). *Equality, Responsibility, and the Law.* Cambridge: Cambridge University Press.

Roemer, J. (1998). *Equality of Opportunity.* Cambridge, Mass.: Harvard University Press.

Ryan, A. (1987). Introduction. In *John Stuart Mill and Jeremy Bentham: Utilitarianism and Other Essays,* Harmondsworth: Penguin, 7–63.

Scanlon, T. M. (1998). *What We Owe to Each Other.* Cambridge, Mass.: Harvard University Press.

Scheffler, S. (1992). Responsibility, Reactive Attitudes, and Liberalism in Philosophy and Politics. *Philosophy and Public Affairs* 21(4): 299–323.

Scheffler, S. (2001). *Boundaries and Allegiances: Problems of Justice and Responsibility in Liberal Thought.* Oxford: Oxford University Press.

Scheffler, S. (2003). What is Egalitarianism? *Philosophy and Public Affairs* 31(1): 5–39.

Scheffler, S. (2005). Choice, Circumstance, and the Value of Equality. *PPE: Politics, Philosophy, and Economics* 4(1): 5–28.

Simester, A. P. and G. R. Sullivan (2003). *Criminal Law: Theory and Doctrine.* Oxford: Hart Publishing.

Slote, M. (1980). Understanding Free Will. *Journal of Philosophy* 77: 136–51.

Smart, J. J. C. (1961). Freewill, Praise, and Blame. *Mind* 70: 291–306.

Stephen, S. J. F. (1883). *A History of the Criminal Law of England*. London: Macmillan.

Strawson, G. (1986). *Freedom and Belief*. London: Methuen.

Strawson, G. (1998). Free-Will. In *The Routledge Encyclopedia of Philosophy*, ed. E. Craig, London: Routledge, 743–53.

Strawson, G. (1999). The Impossibility of Moral Responsibility. In *What Do We Deserve? A Reader on Justice and Desert*, ed. L. P. Pojman and O. McLeod, Oxford: Oxford University Press, 114–24.

Strawson, P. (1962). Freedom and Resentment. *Proceedings of the British Academy* 48: 1–25.

Vuoso, G. (1987). Background, Responsibility, and Excuse. *Yale Law Journal* 96: 1661–86.

Wacquant, L. (2002). Deadly Symbiosis: Rethinking Race and Imprisonment in Twenty-First Century America. *Boston Review* 27(2): 23–31.

Waldron, J. (2002a). *God, Locke, and Equality: Christian Foundations of John Locke's Political Thought*. Cambridge: Cambridge University Press.

Waldron, J. (2002b). Justice. In *Political Science: State of the Discipline (Centennial Edition)*, ed. I. Katznelson and H. V. Milner, New York: W. W. Norton, 266–85.

Wallace, R. J. (1994). *Responsibility and the Moral Sentiments*. Cambridge, Mass., and London: Harvard University Press.

Walzer, M. (1987). *Interpretation and Social Criticism*. Cambridge, Mass., and London: Harvard University Press.

Walzer, M. (1988). *The Company of Critics: Social Criticism and Political Commitment in the Twentieth Century*. New York: Basic Books.

Watson, G. (1987). Responsibility and the Limits of Evil: Reflections on a Strawsonian Theme. In *Responsibility, Character and the Emotions: New Essays in Moral Psychology*, ed. F. Schoeman, Cambridge: Cambridge University Press, 256–86.

Watson, G. (2004). *Agency and Answerability: Selected Essays*, Oxford: Oxford University Press.

Williams, B. A. O. (1993). *Shame and Necessity*. Berkeley and Oxford: University of California Press.

Williams, B. A. O. (1995). Voluntary Acts and Responsible Agents. In *Making Sense of Humanity and Other Philosophical Papers 1982–1993*, Cambridge: Cambridge University Press, 22–34.

Williams, B. A. O. (1997). Moral Responsibility and Political Freedom. *Cambridge Law Journal* 56(1): 96–102.

Wolf, S. (1987). Sanity and the Metaphysics of Responsibility. In *Responsibility, Character, and the Emotions: New Essays in Moral Psychology*, ed. F. Schoeman, Cambridge: Cambridge University Press, 46–62.

Wootton, B. (1963). *Crime and the Criminal Law: Reflections of a Magistrate and Social Scientist*. London: Stevens & Sons.

Wootton, B. (1967). *In a World I Never Made*. London: George Allen & Unwin.

Wootton, B. (1978). *Crime and Penal Policy: Reflections on Fifty Years' Experience*. London: George Allen & Unwin.

Wootton, B. (1959). *Social Science and Social Pathology*. London: Allen & Unwin.

Index

Ajax 53–5
Anderson, E. 72, 77–8, 151
Appiah, A. 84
Aristotle 44, 65
Arneson, R. 71–2, 85, 148, 151
Ashworth, A. 9, 112, 155, 156

Barry, B. 16, 27, 32, 72, 75, 144,
    147, 150, 151, 153
  and semi-choicism 81–4
  on Rawls's argument for
    'democratic equality' 89
Bentham, J. 18
Berlin, I. 4, 68, 109
Blackwell, B. 132–6
Blair, T. 5, 7, 8, 9, 69–70
Brown, G. 6, 7
Burgess, A. 19
Bush, G. 8
Butler, S. 19

Charvet, J. 153
Clinton, W. 5, 7, 8, 69–70,
    146
Clockwork Orange, A 19
Cohen, G. 72, 74–81, 102–5,
    151

compatibilism 26–8
  compared with the
    chance/choice debate 85–6
  Frankfurt's account of 28–30
  mesh accounts of 28–33
  reasons-responsiveness accounts
    of 33–50
Cummins, R. 31

Daniels, N. 62
Dawkins, R. 140–2
Deacon, A. 7, 146
Derbyshire, D. 137
determinism 21–2, 23, 33, 34,
    37–9
distributive justice 2–3
  and equality 15–16, 67, 110
  and retributive justice compared
    116–18, 139
  defined 65–6
Donziger, S. 147, 156
Duff, R. 113, 119, 131
Dworkin, R. 151
  and Cohen on choice and
    chance 74–7, 80–4, 102–5
  and 'option' and 'brute' luck
    102–3

Dworkin, R. (*continued*)
  and responsibility for personality
    82–5, 102–3, 142
  and the political value of
    responsibility-sensitive
    egalitarianism 72–3

excuses 3, 16–17, 115–16, 128
  Wallace on 34–7
expensive tastes 75

fairness-threatening and non-
    fairness-threatening chance
    103–5, 138–9
Fawlty, B. 140
Feinberg, J. 17, 94, 100, 116
Fischer, J. 22, 23, 38, 148
Fischer, J. and Ravizza, M. 148
  account of responsibility 43–50
  and the ahistorical nature of
    mesh compatibilism 29–33,
    38, 48–9
  on Frankfurt 28–9
Frankfurt, H. 22, 28–30, 31, 44
Frankfurt cases 22–3, 45
Friedman, M. 69

Garland, D. 5, 7, 8, 113
Golding, M. 17, 116

Harris, R. 129–30
Hart, H. 58, 122–4, 128, 156
Hayek, F. 69
Hobbes, T. 68
Homes, O. 120–1, 125, 155–6
Hurley, S. 16, 23

incarceration rates 8

James, W. 21, 22

Kagan, S. 154
Kane, R. 45, 48
Kant, I. 4
Kelly, P. 151

Kutz, C. 115, 119
Kymlicka, W. 151, 152, 157
  on Rawls 86–93

Lacey, N. 120

Major, J. 7, 9
Mandle, J. 152, 153
Matravers, M. 16, 93, 114, 142,
    150, 151, 154
Mendus, S. 146, 156
Miller, D. 3
Morse, S. 130, 131–2
Murray, C. 6, 146

Narcissistic Personality Disorder
    (NPD) 133–4
Nagel, T. 4, 152, 153
Nietzsche, F. 15, 100
Nineteen Eighty-Four 19
Nozick, R. 15, 32, 61, 69, 94

Oedipus 52–3, 54, 55
Olsaretti, S. 154
Orwell, G. 19

Personal Responsibility and Work
    Opportunity Reconciliation
    Act 7, 146
Plato 15, 65, 100

Rawls, J. 15, 61, 65, 98–9, 106,
    144–5, 151, 152, 157
  and effort 76
  and equality of opportunity
    87–9
  as not a responsibility-sensitive
    egalitarian 92–6
  Kymlicka's interpretation of
    86–93
  lack of political impact of 68–9
Reagan, R. 5, 7, 68–9
responsibility
  and alternative possibilities 22–3
  and character 29–31, 33

and desert 93–6, 114–19
and determinism 21–22, 23
and politics 5–11, 69–71
and principles of justice 16
and relation to Christianity 4
and 'the Causal Thesis' 24–6
experiencing 20–1
importance in ordinary life 1–2,
4–5
predicted 'withering away' of
17–19
responsibility-sensitive
egalitarianism
and the debate between
Dworkin and Cohen, 74–7
defined 67–8, 71–2
depth problems with 79–80
philosophical and political
appeal of 72–3
width problems with 77–9
retributive justice 3, 93, 111–14
Ripstein, A. 111
Roemer, J. 75, 79

Scanlon, T. 24, 30, 157
Scheffler, S. 73, 80, 83, 106, 116,
151, 152
and the value of equality 96–8
critique of responsibility-
sensitive egalitarianism 78–9
on desert in politics and
philosophy 69–71
on Rawls 94–6
Schroeder, G. 69
semi-choicism 80–4

Simister, A. 135–6, 154, 155
Slote, M. 32, 38
Smart, J. 18–19
Stephen, J. 58, 60, 61, 154–5
Strawson, G. 41–3, 46, 140–2
and compatibilism 26–7
and the basic argument against
moral responsibility 24–6,
31–2, 38, 49, 57
and the problem of free will as a
carousel 50, 63, 86, 132, 150
on experiencing responsibility
20–1
Strawson, P. 1–2, 4, 27, 31, 34, 35,
43, 51, 128
Sullivan, G. 135–6, 154, 155

Thatcher, M. 5, 7, 68–9, 156
'Third Way', the 9

Vuoso, G. 29, 30, 31

Wacquant, L. 147, 156
Waldron, J. 150, 151
Wallace, R. 27, 34, 43, 48–9, 128,
130, 148, 156
account of responsibility 34–42
and Williams on responsibility
54–5
Watson, G. 29, 30, 129–30, 156
Walzer, M. 58–9
Williams, B. 51–60, 112, 150
Wolf, S. 33
Wootton, B. 18–19, 121–2, 125–6,
134, 148, 156